Why Your Bike Is Made in Asia

My Career in Bicycles as I Watched Two Continents Squander an Industry

Bill McGann

Mcgann
Publishing

©2024 Bill McGann
All Rights Reserved

No part of this publication may be reproduced, stored in a retrieval system, or transmitted, in any form or by any means, electronic, mechanical, photocopying, recording, or otherwise, without the written permission of the author.

Published by McGann Publishing
P.O. Box 864
McMinnville, OR 97128
USA
www.mcgannpublishing.com

McGann
Publishing

ISBN 978-1-7367494-1-8
Printed in the United States of America

Table of Contents

Acknowledgements 5
Preface: The Beginning 7
Introduction 9
1. Qu'est-ce que c'est "squeak"? 11
2. The boom hides the rot 35
3. Asian suppliers get a foothold 49
4. Howie ignites the tinder 53
5. Selling Brand X 69
6. Kids really want to play on their bikes 85
7. Moving from retailer to wholesaler 95
8. Twelve years after 113
9. Heading into the 1990s 125
10. The industry moves to Asia 131
Bibliography 145
Index 147

Acknowledgements

I would still be working on this book if I had not received so much help from so many generous people. In particular I must thank writer Peter Joffre Nye, who went over the text and made many valuable suggestions. His own writing about bicycle history is listed in the bibliography. The late Howie Cohen, both an industry pioneer and bicycle business heavyweight, was unstinting in his help. His insights were a crucial contribution.

Two books must be mentioned. Judith Crown and Glenn Coleman's *No Hands—The Rise and Fall of the Schwinn Bicycle Company, An American Institution* remains the finest history of that iconic maker of America's bicycles. Frank Berto's *The Dancing Chain: The History and Development of the Derailleur Bicycle* is an excellent explanation of the subject by the man who knows it best.

Whenever I had a question, always, the people in the bicycle industry were kind and helpful to me. My gratitude to them all is profound.

Any errors are my own.

Preface
The Beginning

The great bike boom was going bust, though no one seemed to know that catastrophe was lurking around the corner. I certainly didn't.

Completely ignorant of what was going on around me, I opened the brilliantly named Bill's Bike Shop on June 1, 1974, probably the day the second great American bike boom ended. From the late 1960s to the early 1970s, importers in the U.S. sent huge orders to bicycle factories around the world. The bicycle industry struggled to fill the insatiable American demand for two-wheeled transport.

That June there were already two retailers of quality bicycles in my town. The local sporting goods shop, with its beautiful wood paneling and high ceilings, carried all the best brands: Adidas, Maharajah, Browning, Voit, Rawlings, Everlast and of course, Schwinn Bicycles.

Across town was the Camarillo Bicycle Center, a busy and well-stocked shop owned by a charming middle-aged man whom I knew only as Chuck. He had all the famous imported lightweights: among them Peugeot, Motobecane and Raleigh. But his top-selling brand was a bike I was barely familiar with, Nishiki, made in Japan. Chuck had populated my town with hundreds and hundreds, possibly thousands of bright orange Nishiki Olympic bikes, Nishiki's basic consumer ten-speed.

Chuck said his Nishikis were not only a terrific value and well-made, they were equipped with wonderfully reliable, cutting-edge derailleurs. He was adamant that Nishiki bikes shouldn't be confused with the shoddy post-war Japanese merchandise everyone thought was junk.

The Schwinn dealer argued that customers were best off with Schwinn because of its well-earned reputation for quality. Schwinn's guarantee carried a no-time-limit warranty that was honored without quibble. To ensure its bikes were assembled and serviced correctly, every Schwinn dealer was encouraged to have its mechanics factory-trained.

My starting inventory was lean, just ten French Gitane ten-speeds and twenty-five Maserati bicycles. The Maseratis were made in Italy by a

McGann

member of the famous car family who used the legendary name to brand his bikes. I told customers my European bikes were light, handled best, and were the product of a cycling culture that demanded good-riding bikes.

Being twenty-two and sorely lacking judgment, I heaped contempt upon Chuck's Nishikis, calling them "Jap Scrap". I felt righteous selling my French and Italian bikes and succeeded well enough that about six months after I opened my shop, I attended Camarillo Bicycle Center's bankruptcy auction. The bike boom was by now long gone and there wasn't enough room for all of us.

But I was wrong and Chuck was right.

How that came to be and what followed is my story.

Introduction

This is a story about an industry that affects nearly every human being on this planet. Bicycles are everywhere, and for good reason. They provide low-cost transportation and employment. They let people get low-impact exercise, to compete, and even enjoy watching professional bike racing as it is televised around the world. Our tale covers three continents, countless manufacturers and dealers, and more than a century of history.

Our history starts in Europe, where the bike was invented, but very soon bicycles were being made and ridden in the New World. On both continents there were several companies whose brands over time became synonymous with quality and desirability. In my own early days in the trade, people had to have certain brands, like Peugeot and Schwinn, with almost no questions asked. Schwinn had done such a fine job of producing well-made bikes that were exactly what the American consumer wanted; for some people the name "Schwinn" became almost interchangeable with "bicycle".

And then, in the face of the extraordinary demand for adult bicycles in the early 1970s and desperate to take advantage of an incredible opportunity to cash in, many esteemed European and American makers ramped up their production, forgetting the focus on quality and innovative design that put them in the forefront of their trade in the first place.

But this was not happening in a vacuum. Bicycles are made nearly everywhere on this planet and in Japan, there were makers particularly dedicated to producing well-made bikes. When these bikes hit the American market, many shop owners quickly dropped the lower-quality western production in favor of the better made, and still competitively priced Asian bikes.

My own shop was a case in point. I had a Euro-centric shop stocked with English, French and Italian bikes until a salesman brought me a Japanese-made Centurion 10-speed to examine and test. The bike was nearly flawless. Very quickly I closed out my lower quality European bikes and had a shop full of Centurions. The result: I made more money and had happier customers.

My experience was replicated thousands of times in shops everywhere.

1
Qu'est-ce que c'est "squeak"?

In 1972 and 1973, former Olympic bicycle racer Chuck Pranke put on the Grand Prix of the United States at the Encino, California, velodrome (an oval, banked bicycle track). Pranke, an extremely likable entrepreneur, had also been a successful bodybuilder, gracing the covers of several muscle magazines in the early 1960s, as well as being 1961 Mr. Los Angeles.

Pranke had broached his idea of staging this international track meet in Los Angeles to former racer Ron Packham. Packham had been vacationing in Israel when he heard from Pranke and immediately dropped what he was doing and traveled to France to talk to one of cycling's most famous cycling coaches, Louis "Toto" Gérardin. The coach had been cycling's 1930 world sprint champion and is said to have received his nickname from famed singer Edith Piaf, who had deeply loved the racer.

Gérardin immediately liked the idea and promised to bring Daniel Morelon and Pierre Trentin, two of the greatest track stars of the age, to the event. He was so taken by the plan he recommended the meet to other world-class European track stars.

A few days later Packham was in Pranke's Santa Monica home telling him, "I have the French." As *Sports Illustrated* writer Larry Keith put it, "If Pranke had been promoting a finger-painting contest, the promise of Picasso would have had no greater impact."

Pranke ended up bringing over several of the world's finest track racers: Germans, Soviets, Canadians, Americans and Frenchmen, including that many-times world sprint champion Daniel Morelon of France.

Because some of France's best were competing, several executives from the Peugeot bicycle company (which was sponsoring the Grand Prix) traveled to the U.S. in 1973 to visit bike shops, see the races and meet with their western U.S. importer.

McGann

At the time, French bike companies exercised a lot of control over their French dealers. Not understanding the consumer-driven, bottom-up nature of American economic power, during their bike shop tour they outraged the independent American Peugeot dealers by telling them they should clean up their displays, put more Peugeot bikes on the floor, and fix the myriad other failings they spotted (at that time, to my knowledge, only Schwinn and Raleigh required signed dealer agreements). Several furious owners threw the uncomprehending Frenchmen out of their stores and called the Peugeot distributor, United Bicycle Sales, and told them to keep those bossy meddlers out of their shops.

The Peugeot entourage had also stopped at nearby Redondo Beach, a coastal town just south of the Los Angeles airport. The beach is famous for its big, well-formed waves that draw hundreds of dedicated surfers as well as scores of beach-volleyball players. Amid this classic Southern California beach scene they watched casual riders cruise by on the cement bike path that followed the coastline.

Many of the cyclists were riding upright on 10-speed bikes with the handlebars turned up, a common practice at the time when out-of-shape riders new to cycling discovered how uncomfortable a dropped-bar bike could be. The Peugeot executives were horrified at the cycling sacrilege.

They arrived at a Los Angeles Airport hotel to meet with United Bicycle's American staff. At the time Peugeot was the hottest import brand and the $149.00 Peugeot UO8, despite its outdated plastic derailleurs and noisy brakes, was a genuine status symbol. I was told that the East Coast Peugeot importer had so much business he would only take orders for full container loads of bikes, a huge commitment for any bicycle shop. But that made it easy for the distributor. The container was simply unloaded from the ship and sent to the dealer along with a giant invoice, creating a huge profit for the distributor. In the west, shipments of Peugeot bikes were sold out long before they arrived.

But, amid this sellers' paradise, the people at United were concerned. They knew the UO8 was badly dated and was selling well only because it was in fashion, an advantage that could end at any time. They also knew other companies were making bikes that more closely fit the real needs of casual American riders.

One of United's staff recalled the meeting. "Business is good", the French Peugeot executives were told, "and if we make a few inexpensive changes to keep American buyers happy, we can preserve our place in the market for a while longer.

Why Your Bike Is Made in Asia

"First, most retail customers immediately replace the uncomfortable hard leather saddle with a padded plastic one. If we put on an inexpensive soft saddle, we can remove a sales objection and lower the cost of the bike.

"Also, the sticker on the head tube doesn't look good to an American. It should be replaced with an embossed badge. And even more important, Americans don't like bending down to the handlebar drops to reach the brake levers. Peugeot bikes should come with brake extension levers so they can slow their bikes while holding the tops of the bars."

During their visit to the Redondo Beach bike path the Peugeot people had witnessed the reason for the last request. Yet all three suggestions were shot down, mostly in the name of preserving Peugeot's proud racing heritage.

There was a last suggestion. "Peugeots come with Mafac center-pull brakes which leave ugly black rubber deposits on the rims and squeak horribly. We should use a quieter brake."

The head Frenchman looked quizzically at the American making the presentation and twisted his head in seeming puzzlement and asked, "*Qu'est-ce que c'est* squeak?" [What does "squeak" mean?]

It was a telling moment. The Peugeot executive had treated an earnest customer's intelligent request with contempt. Not for a second did anyone in the room believe this was the first time he had heard about squealing Mafac brakes. Even the rankest amateur mechanic knew Mafac brakes were wonderfully powerful, but it was almost impossible to silence their deafening screech. I remember a good French amateur telling me of his racing days in early 1960s France. He recalled that when a large pack would descend mountain passes, everyone could smell the stink of the cheap Mafac pads as the brakes heated, as well as the unbelievable howl a large peloton equipped with Mafac brakes could make.

But pretense or not, the bike boom was still raging in 1973 and Peugeot was selling every bike they could make. After the meeting, the UO8 remained unchanged.

It wasn't always this way. For decades French bike companies were brilliant innovators. When those Mafac brakes were introduced at the 1952 Paris bike show, they were the first classic center-pull and were a fabulous advance over the poor-stopping side-pulls of the time. They required so little effort their tag line was, "One finger is enough."

Important to cyclists of the time, they were powerful and their design still allowed large frame clearances for fenders and mud. Through a quirk of physics, bigger clearances for fenders means side-pull brakes need longer arms to reach past the fenders to the rims, giving them less mechanical advantage and thus less stopping power. This is also true of center-pull brakes, but because their design lowers the caliper pivot points so that they are closer to the rim, this tendency is minimized. In the 1950s, dirt roads were far from unknown in Europe and on a rainy day a bike without fenders could get fouled with mud to the point of being unrideable.

For a time, Mafac center-pull brakes were the state-of-the art and were used by the world's finest racers, such as five-time Tour de France winner Jacques Anquetil. Other big brake makers, notably Weinmann of Switzerland and Universal of Italy, didn't come out with center-pulls until the late 1950s and early 1960s.

Jacques Anquetil and Raymond Poulidor in stage 20 of the 1964 Tour de France

In fact, going back to cycling's beginnings, it was a Frenchman who invented the true bicycle.

But first, let's put a wooden stake in the heart of an oft-repeated story of the bicycle's origin. The story goes that the first bike, called a *célérifère*, was made by a Count Mède de Sivrac in 1790. He is said to have joined two wheels with a horse-shaped wooden frame. The rider was closer to the ground than with a modern bicycle and could then walk along briskly, the frame supporting his weight. We now know that this is untrue, there was no such count and the story was a hoax perpetrated by late nineteenth century journalist Louis Baudry de Saunier. Though long-disproved, this

Why Your Bike Is Made in Asia

is a canard that will not die and continues to be repeated. It was even in a book put out by the 1976 Montreal Olympic Games organizer.

The first modestly successful two-wheeler was in fact invented by Baron Karl von Drais. Drais had a job as forestry master for the Grand Duchy of Baden in southwest Germany (though the country that we know as Germany had not yet come into existence). This was a position that his father had secured for him that allowed Drais time to work on his inventions.

For years he had been trying to make a practical human-powered transport machine. His earlier efforts culminated in 1813 with a four-wheeler that could carry as many as four people and was propelled by a servant in the back powering the rear wheels with foot planks that could crank the axle. Drais was unable to either excite people about his machine nor could he secure a patent for it.

Despite this initial lack of success, as far has human-powered transport was concerned, Drais was not about to give up.

Drais' next stab at getting down the road was a device initially called a "laufmaschine" (running machine) and later, using his name, "draisine". A draisine looked much like a modern bicycle and importantly it could be steered with a tiller that allowed the rider to turn the front wheel. There were no pedals. As was said about the célérifère, the rider sat on the saddle and walked or ran down the road with his weight supported by the draisine's saddle.

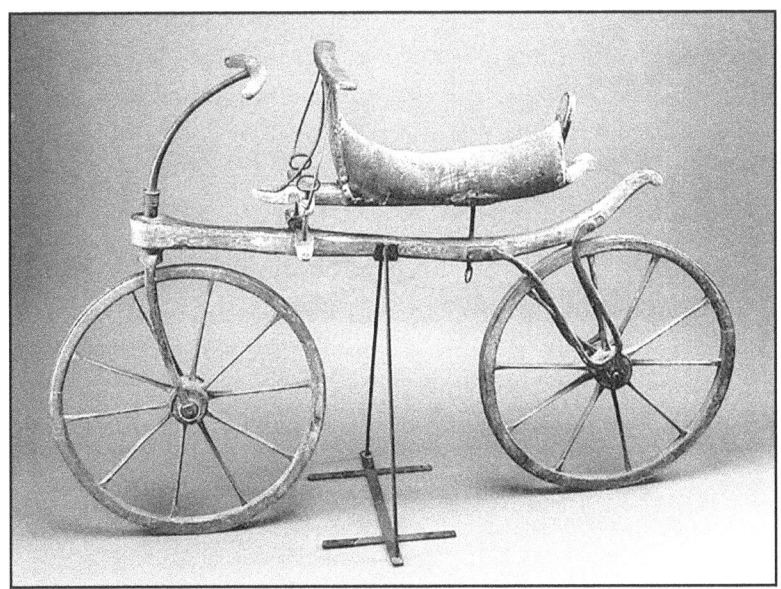

The 1818 Draisine

On a flat smooth road (far less common in the early nineteenth century than today), a draisine rider could easily go along at a running pace with just a modest effort. This 1817 invention had an initial burst of popularity; the French government even supplied some to postmen. But its fundamental impracticality, especially given the roads of the time, killed its commercial potential. Climbing hills was nearly impossible and descending was dangerous. Milan, in what is now bike-mad Italy (the unified country of Italy did not exist at that time, either), initially banned draisines.

Though there were many attempts during the first half of the nineteenth century to improve the draisine and make it practical, it would be another forty years before human power could be properly harnessed to move a vehicle down the road.

There is one surviving relic of the draisine, its French name is still used for bikes: Velocipede, made from the French words for speed and foot.

In 1862 nineteen-year-old Pierre Lallement saw a rider go by on a draisine, by now a strange sight of a long-discarded device. At the time, our Frenchman was living in Nancy and working in a shop that built baby carriages. Lallement pondered the device and had the brilliant insight to put pedals on a crank, and that crank on the front wheel. Now living in Paris and with the help of fellow shop workers, his idea was turned into a working machine. Voila! The bicycle (then weighing seventy pounds) was born.

Lallement had a passing involvement with the Olivier brothers, Aimé, René, and Marius. The Oliviers partnered with Ernest Michaux (who later falsely claimed to have invented the bicycle) and began producing these pedaled vehicles. But it was early days and the bikes Michaux and the Oliviers produced weren't ready for commercial production. Most important, the frames were initially made of cast iron and were not only prone to breakage, at the time there was no existing technology that could repair them. In 1868, recognizing the need to improve their product, they changed to an improved frame design and made it of wrought iron.

By the end of the decade the Oliviers successfully sued to dissolve the partnership. The brothers, with René in charge, took over the factory with a new company, *Compagnie Parisienne*. Legal changes to company ownership could not change the fact that the initial European and American enthusiasm for the two-wheeled machines had faded. The wood or iron-framed, steel-wheeled bike wasn't ready to be a reliable, widely used tool of transportation.

Lallement moved to the U.S. in 1865 with two of his bikes as part of his luggage and while living in Ansonia, Connecticut, he further refined his invention.

Why Your Bike Is Made in Asia

He was recognized as the bicycle's inventor by the U.S. Patent office, which granted him Patent Number 59,915 on November 20, 1866, for "Improvement in Velocipedes". This was the first American bicycle-related patent. It would not be the last. Historian David Herlihy has made a compelling case that Lallement, not Michaux, is the man who changed the world.

Unable to find an American manufacturer interested in producing his invention, in 1868 Lallement returned to France. At some point he went back to the U.S. and sold his bicycle patent (which expired in 1883) to Albert Pope. Albert Pope's Pope Manufacturing Company will play a large part in our story.

Pierre Lallemant and his velocipede

Another Frenchman, Eugene Meyer (actually living in France), adapted the tensioned wire or spoked wheel for bicycles, receiving a patent for this improvement in 1869. Until this invention, a wheel was made with a wooden hub, spokes and rim. A heated iron band was put over the rims. As the iron rim cooled, it would shrink, compressing everything into a usable, sturdy wheel. This might have been acceptable for cart wheels, but it was heavy and difficult to repair.

Meyer's brilliant insight made possible a strong, light wheel that could be used both on the high wheelers of the 1870s and 1880s as well as modern bicycles. Using his tension wheel, Meyer produced bicycles that weighed about forty-four pounds, around twenty pounds lighter than bikes with wood-steel compression wheels.

After Lallement and Meyer, the British made many of the great advances that changed Lallement's barely rideable toy into a practical transport tool for the masses. In 1869 at London's Crystal Palace, British maker Reynolds & May showed a steel-framed bike with a large front wheel, or high-wheeler, with rubber tires mounted on its steel rims.

Things moved quickly. By the early 1870s, all-metal frames and wheels with solid rubber tires were widely available. The front wheel grew ever larger, extending the distance a rider could travel with each rotation of the cranks. Eventually bike makers were producing front wheels that were about 5 feet in diameter (1.5 meters). That was the era's only way to give a bicycle the equivalent of a higher gear (greater distance traveled with each rotation of the pedal cranks).

Mounting and riding one of these splendid, tall machines was difficult and hazardous. Because of their huge front wheels and small trailing wheels, the name "penny-farthing" (for the large and small British coins) was used to describe the highwheeler bicycle of the late 1870s. The ride of these early bicycles was so rough, people took to calling them "boneshakers", a name that stuck through most of the nineteenth century.

In 1885 Englishman John Kemp Starley revolutionized the bicycle industry, which was then primarily devoted to supplying well-to-do sportsmen. Starley's firm, Starley & Sutton Co., was dedicated to developing a bicycle that was safe to ride. He made the dangerous highwheeler obsolete when he created the modern, chain-drive to rear wheel "safety bicycle" with (almost) equal-sized front and rear wheels. Though there were earlier attempts to cure the high-wheeler's problems with smaller wheels, it was Starley's Rover bicycle that changed cycling.

It wasn't quite like a modern bicycle. The Rover had a 30-inch diameter rear wheel—smaller than the 36-inch front wheel—and it had a complex lever-actuated steering mechanism. Though heavier than the dominant penny-farthings, it was faster because of the rider's smaller frontal area, which dramatically reduced wind drag.

Starley listened to both the complaints about his bike and as well as suggestions on how to improve it and was soon making bikes with simple direct steering (the fork and handlebar assembly was hinged on the head tube), and forks with rake (forward bend) to soften the ride and give the front wheel caster to make riding a straight line easier. The bike had a brake lever on the handlebar that forced a pad to press against the top of the front wheel. His 1885 Rover was simpler, better and practical.

Why Your Bike Is Made in Asia

Now there was a bike everyone could ride.

Women joyously embraced the new bicycle and the liberation it bestowed. Susan B. Anthony made this feeling clear when she said, "She who succeeds in gaining the mastery of the bicycle will gain the mastery of life."

The Starley Rover bicycle. Photo credit: Karen Roe, under Creative Commons Attribution 2.0 Generic license.

Bikes were made on both sides of the Atlantic. In the United States, Albert H. Overman started his bicycle company in Chicopee Falls, Massachusetts in 1882, his first product being a three-wheeler. Being a good businessman, he also made high-wheelers.

When Starley's safety bicycle made its appearance, unlike other American bicycle manufacturers who resisted this innovation, Overman instantly understood that this was the bicycle of the future and by 1888 he was turning out high-quality safety bicycles under the Victor name.

They were better than any other bicycle for several reasons. He had no cast parts, his frames were what we now call a diamond frame, made with a front and rear triangle. On his steel rims he mounted a hollow rubber "cushion tire". Wonderfully, his bikes were made with interchangeable parts so that it could be easily repaired.

Overman looked to be set. At its height his company had 1,400 employees working in five buildings turning out 80,000 bikes a year. In the

McGann

mid-1890s, demand for bicycles exploded, and the first great bike boom was underway.

But, it didn't last. Overman got into a huge legal fight with his distributor, the Spalding sports equipment company. An endless fight with his distributor, along with many other makers entering the business with lower-priced bikes while the bike boom was ending, Overman's dream

Elegant advertising poster for the Victor Bicycle Company

Why Your Bike Is Made in Asia

turned into a nightmare. He was deeply in debt when a fire broke out in his factory on November 10, 1899. The remains of the firm were sold soon thereafter.

Scotsman John Dunlop developed and patented a pneumatic tire that could be glued onto a bicycle rim, but it was Frenchman Édouard Michelin who made a big leap toward greater practicality when he introduced the detachable, or "clincher" bicycle tire.

Historian Peter Joffre Nye has detailed the interesting complexity of the clincher tire's triumph in his book, *The Fast Times of Albert Champion*. Though Dunlop had indeed, developed the first practical pneumatic bicycle tire, it was Robert W. Thompson who was the true inventor of the air-filled tire. Back in 1845, the English Patent Office had issued the Scotsman a patent for pneumatic tires that were to be used on horse-drawn carriage wheels. No one bought his tires and the idea sank with little trace. The discovery of the earlier and now-expired Thompson patent invalidated Dunlop's, allowing the Michelins to proceed with developing and marketing their clinchers.

Now the marketplace was faced with two tire designs, the Dunlop and the Michelin. The fight was settled in the arena of sport. Working for the Parisian blue-collar newspaper *Le Petit Journal*, Pierre Giffard organized an extraordinary bicycle race, Paris–Brest–Paris, in 1891. It was 750 miles (1,200 kilometers) that took the riders from Paris almost to the far western tip of the Breton peninsula and back to Paris. The excitement Giffard's race created was extraordinary.

After more than seventy-one sleepless hours of riding over late nineteenth-century roads, rider Charles Terront's English Humber bicycle with Michelin tires rolled across the finish line first. Second-place Pierre Jiel-Laval on Dunlop rubber needed eight more hours to reach Paris. Importantly, the first two finishers were on pneumatic tires.

Because this race had transfixed the cycling world's attention, effectively, two product wars were over. The solid rubber tire quickly died, and the Michelins, brilliantly exploiting Terront's victory, gained a huge marketing advantage for their clincher tires. Eventually most of the cycling world would adopt the clincher design. As we'll see, one important market—the U.S.—resisted.

A way to accurately mass-produce ball-bearings was another crucial late-nineteenth century development, as were roller chains and higher-strength steel tubing. In 1897 the Reynolds Tube Company patented a method to butt steel bicycle tubes: make the steel tubes thicker at the ends where more strength was needed at the joints and thinner in the center.

This makes the tube lighter and the resulting bike more comfortable. Metal bicycle tubes for high-performance steel bikes are still butted using the technology developed by Reynolds in the nineteenth century, though competitive riders now usually use carbon-fiber frames.

The first bikes with chain-drive to rear wheel were hampered by the primitive chains of the era. Modern low-friction bush-roller chains didn't show up until 1898.

By the late 1800s, with the exception of caliper brakes (although a patent had been issued for caliper brakes in 1887) and derailleurs, bicycles as we know them were being ridden by millions of people all over the world. British bikes were particularly prized, even by the French (like Terront). In America, great factories pumped out vast numbers of two-wheelers for a population eager to travel.

The nineteenth century's second industrial revolution was in full swing and the bicycle was the recipient of many of its innovations, among them: Bessemer steel, rubber, and efficient transport through improved railroads and steamships. By the end of the nineteenth century the United States had issued 7,573 patents for bicycles and items associated with cycling.

The great bike boom showed serious signs of slowing in 1897 and by 1898, bikes were being dumped by both manufacturers and retailers. America's first great bike boom was over.

For centuries, the Peugeot family, French Protestants who had been exiled for a time to Switzerland for their religious beliefs, made their living as farmers and millers in Franche-Comte, near the Swiss border. In 1810 Jean-Pierre and Jean-Frédéric Peugeot made the fateful decision to use one of the family's mills to make metal castings. While the casting trade wasn't profitable, the family persisted in the metals business and began making springs for the nearby clock and watch industry. The hard-working Peugeots prospered, quickly going into cold-rolling, and shortly thereafter, hot-rolling steel. They expanded the family enterprise, using their metalworking expertise to make saws and tools for agriculture. Ever widening their product base, the Peugeots even made corset stays. One of their nineteenth-century product home-runs was a table-top coffee grinder, which remained a Peugeot manufacturing mainstay for many decades. By the French Second Empire (1852–1870, when France was ruled by Napoleon III) the Peugeot company was rich, successful and well-run.

The business was always managed by a direct male descendent of Jean-Jacques Peugeot, a miller born in 1699. It wasn't until 1966 that the family appointed a chief executive who wasn't a Peugeot.

Why Your Bike Is Made in Asia

A scion of the Peugeot family who had studied engineering at the elite École Central Paris (as had Gustav Eiffel and André Michelin), Armand Peugeot had spent much of his life in Leeds, England and had seen how popular the highwheeler had become. In 1882 he talked his family into opening a factory in Montbéliard with 300 workers to make high-wheelers and then, later, tricycles. Peugeot was quick to begin producing safety bicycles, jumping into production the same year (1885) that Starley introduced his revolutionary design. By 1900, Peugeot was making 20,000 bicycles a year in a factory Armand opened in Beaulieu, where Peugeot would make bicycles into the late twentieth century. Meanwhile, the Peugeot family also began manufacturing cars. Over the decades, the various arms of Peugeot businesses would separate and re-merge and today they are under one financial umbrella.

Peugeot also realized that sponsoring the best bicycle riders was the most effective way to popularize the brand. Hiring not only the strongest riders, Peugeot's team was managed by some of the best directors in the history of the sport. Always run with a brutal frugality, riders nicknamed the early Peugeot team *Le Taule* (The Prison). Into the 1970s, Peugeot riders were poorly paid and even had to buy their own cycling socks. Yet, by the time the professional team folded in 1986, riders on Peugeot bikes had won the Tour de France ten times.

Early twentieth century racers in France and Italy preferred single-speed fixed-gear bikes with their efficient direct connection between the crank and the rear wheel. The Tour de France, a power unto itself, didn't allow derailleurs on bikes ridden by sponsored professionals until 1937. But French cyclo-tourists wanted to travel everywhere on their bikes and craved reliable machines with good brakes and gear-changing systems. Every athlete's body is different, but the majority of riders are most efficient if they turn the pedals in the seventy-five to eighty-five rpm range. That means different gear ratios are needed for hills, head and tail winds, as well as good and bad roads. With the availability of a range of gear ratios, a rider can maintain that optimum cadence.

Before the First World War, French inventors had already developed practical production rear derailleurs (gear changers). Joanny Panel's 1911 *Le Chemineau* (The Tramp) derailleur solved all of the fundamental problems plaguing earlier gear-change system designers, and was sufficiently advanced that Panel was able to produce and sell the same basic design until 1949.

McGann

Why was France the hotbed of bicycle touring? Writer Raymond Henry explained that France had a large middle class with both money and leisure time, was blessed with good roads, temperate climate and a varied terrain that inspired Frenchmen to take to the road and explore their country. They organized clubs, and these cycle-touring clubs were in no small part the source of innovation and drive to improve the bicycle. The clubs held

Joanny Panel's 1911 Le Chemineau rear derailleur. Photo credit: Colin, onlinebicyclemuseum.co.uk

sophisticated trials to test and vet innovations in their search for lightweight bikes that would carry a demanding and dedicated cyclist anywhere he wanted to go.

French businessmen worked hard to satisfy this demand. Albert Raimond, who earlier had been a manager at the same firm where Panel had worked before setting out on his own, began making Cyclo derailleurs in the 1920s. Bicycle tourists all over Europe bought them, making Cyclo the first big-selling derailleur.

Dijon bike shop owner Lucien Juy started making Simplex-brand derailleurs in 1928 and by 1933 was selling 40,000 units a year. In 1936 he was moving 1,000 derailleurs a day. Simplex was first to spring-load the top of the derailleur where it attached to the frame to keep the chain properly tensioned. This is a basic design requirement of all modern derailleurs. Juy was also the first to use a $3/32$" chain, the world standard for derailleur bikes until the start of the twenty-first century. Juy was a gifted promoter who

Why Your Bike Is Made in Asia

made sure that whenever possible, the best professional riders used his equipment. Both Raimond and Juy did so well they set up factories outside France, Raimond (Cyclo) in England and Juy (Simplex) in Italy.

An important future protagonist, André Huret, began producing derailleurs in 1930 but his pre-war market penetration was miniscule.

Bicycle rims for tubular, or "sew up" tires (the casing is wrapped and sewn around the tube and the resulting tire is glued to the rim) were made of wood until French firm Mavic came up with a practical aluminum rim in 1926. Again fighting a losing war against technology, the Tour de France forbade the use of aluminum rims until the 1930s. Some racers, like 1931 and 1934 Tour winner Antonin Magne, would paint their Mavic aluminum rims to look like wood to fool Tour officials.

In the mid-1930s (no one is exactly sure exactly when) French crankset maker Stronglight developed the cotterless crankset. Until then (and on nearly all bikes long after) cranks were secured to the bottom bracket axle with a nutted tapered-steel cotter. No mechanic from the 1960s and '70s misses the effort spent removing rusted or deformed crank cotters from European consumer bikes, nor the job of finding and/or filing a new cotter to make the right and left crank arms line up. Good shops had a huge assortment of cotters of different diameters, lengths and tapers because almost every country and sometimes it seemed every crank manufacturer needed a different one.

With a cotterless crank, the mechanic need only use the proper extractor to pull the crank from the tapered steel axle. Replacing it was a cinch: just press the crank on the spindle and tighten the fixing bolt. It would be forty years before this superior design made its way to European consumer bikes, and though it was a French invention, French bike companies were reluctant to use them. It was a truculence that would cost them dearly.

French makers centered their industry in city of St. Etienne, in east-central France, not far from Lyon. St. Etienne became home to almost one hundred firms making components and bikes. The pre-war bicycle industry was big. Peugeot made and sold 162,000 bikes in 1930, up from 80,000 in the years before the First World War. French factories continually improved their products through the 1930s. With the resumption of production after the Second World War, the bicycle industry's ferocious competitiveness kept makers constantly tinkering, often updating their products yearly. The immediate postwar years were a wonderful time to be in the bicycle business in Europe. The war-ravaged continent needed wheels and a bicycle was the cheapest and most sensible solution. The Milan bicycle show never had more attendees than in 1947.

McGann

Bicycle companies, especially those of Italy and France, were rich and ambitious. They poured money into professional racing, creating what is now called bike racing's Golden Age. Peugeot's sales climbed to 220,000 bikes a year. At the time, only companies within the bicycle industry were allowed to sponsor professional bicycle racing teams.

It was a time when some of the sport's greatest legends raced on a continent whose countries were finally learning how to get along. The once-high duties that made each country a separate market fell with the advent of the European Common Market in 1957. There was still fierce nationalistic pride, but it was, in the words of cycle historian Jean-Paul Ollivier, "…a good rivalry. France, Italy, Belgium, Spain, they all had their champions." It was a competition to excel, not annihilate.

In 1950, Italian genius tinkerer, inventor and craftsman Tullio Campagnolo came out with his second truly great product, the Gran Sport rear derailleur. Earlier, he had been credited with inventing the quick-release hub. With the flick of a lever rather than fussing with wing nuts, a rider could remove his wheel. The quick-release was a complex and brilliant advance that alone would have given the Italian immortality. But before we move on, let's take a closer look at the quick release.

Here is the official story: The Campagnolo component company got its start in 1927 when a reasonably successful amateur racer named Gentullio Campagnolo was racing in the Gran Premio della Vittoria. On that November 11, "Tullio" Campagnolo was crossing the Croce d'Aune pass and needed to change gears. In those days, that meant loosening the rear wheel so that the chain could be moved manually to a different size rear cog.

But this was November in the high Dolomite mountains, part of the southern Alps. At 3,300 feet (1,015 meters), Campagnolo couldn't loosen the frozen wing nuts securing his rear wheel. He famously said to himself, "*Bisogna cambià qualcossa de drio*" (the dialect of his hometown Vicenza for "*Bisogna cambiare qualcosa dietro*"), or "something must be changed in the rear." Though Campagnolo did finish fourth in that race, what followed has affected nearly every rider of lightweight bikes: he invented the quick-release hub skewer. With the flip of a lever, the wheel is loosened or tightened almost instantly.

In 1930 Campagnolo patented his brilliant invention and was soon having a local machine shop make his hubs.

Well…historians have gone back and looked again at the story. They find no record of a Gran Premio della Vittoria race in the Dolomites that November, though there was one in 1925. And further, it is asserted

Why Your Bike Is Made in Asia

that there is no 1930 Campagnolo patent for the quick-release. Modern historians say Campagnolo's quick-release patents are for improvements on an existing device.

In any case, by the mid-1930s Campagnolo was exporting his hubs, which were not particularly superior to his competition, except they had his superb quick release. Still, growth was slow. He didn't hire his first full-time employee until 1940.

It was after the war that Campagnolo's fertile genius (and he was a genius, let there be no doubt about that) and desire to make the world's finest parts caused the company to become the well-known and revered company it is today.

Up until 1950, Campagnolo gear-changing systems were supremely efficient and staggeringly difficult to use. Campagnolo advanced derailleur design decades ahead with his Gran Sport, a sturdy brass vertical parallelogram that deformed with the pull of single wire to move the chain across the rear cogset (he had made a two-cable parallelogram rear derailleur in 1949). In 1951 Swiss racer Hugo Koblet won the Tour de France using Campagnolo derailleurs.

With some important changes, this is basically how a derailleur works today. It was a beautiful work of genius, but like all of Campagnolo's precision handmade products, the Gran Sport was too expensive to use on production bikes. It wasn't until 1958, with the introduction of French company Huret's Allvit, that a low-cost deforming parallelogram derailleur was produced. Simplex followed suit in 1961.

Campagnolo did not invent the parallelogram rear derailleur. There were several introduced just before the war, notably the French Nivex and Spirex changers, which shifted superbly, better than Campagnolo's early designs. There were also pre-war patents awarded to Italian inventor Francesco Ghiggini for a parallelogram rear derailleur. Historian Frank Berto credits Ghiggini with the original design of the Gran Sport, noting that Campagnolo bought Ghiggini's patents in 1951. It is my guess that Campagnolo felt (or was informed) that his designs infringed on Ghiggini's patents and writing the inventor a check was the simplest solution.

Campagnolo's simple, elegant Gran Sport represented an enormous advance in reliability, usability and simplicity. We remember his design because it was just better than all the others.

The big players in the post-war derailleur business were Simplex and Huret. What were they making that was inferior to Campagnolo's Gran Sport changer?

McGann

After the war, Simplex, Huret and Cyclo produced rear derailleurs that used a coiled flat spring to both keep the chain tensioned and help move the chain across the sprockets. A cable through the center of the spring would pull the jockey/tensioner to the desired cog. These are generally called "plunger-type" derailleurs. Cyclo derailleurs used two cables.

Both British and French Cyclo companies decided the freewheel business was friendlier and concentrated their efforts there, though both firms produced their pre-war rear derailleurs into the early 1960s. French Cyclo began making a single-cable plunger derailleur in 1962, but soon thereafter the company stopped producing derailleurs. British Cyclo introduced a parallelogram derailleur in 1961, but a few years later the firm exited the changer business.

Cyclo's Benelux rear derailleur. Photo credit: Classic Cycle, Bainbridge Island, WA.

Despite the superiority of Campagnolo's derailleurs, Louison Bobet won three Tours de France as well as the French and World Championships in the early to mid-1950s, riding Stella bikes mounted with plunger-type Huret derailleurs. In the end, it is the legs.

Through the 1950s and beyond, Europe remained crazy about bike racing, but became less enthusiastic about actually owning bicycles and using them for transportation. As the postwar recovery started to take hold, Europeans began riding Vespa scooters and driving Fiat Topolinos

Why Your Bike Is Made in Asia

and Citroën 2CVs. All three were superb engineering examples that made motorized transport affordable to a wide swath of Europeans enjoying the economic rebirth. The Citroën 2CV, with its distinctive canvas sunroof, was so well designed that it was produced from 1948 until 1990. This proved to be hard competition for the bicycle.

During the late 1940s, the French bought 1.3 million bikes a year, a third again more than the industry's best pre-war year, 1938. Ominously, in 1952 the number fell to 750,000 and 1957's sales were 534,000. This trend was mimicked all over Europe.

The crashing bike sales spelled danger for the glamorous, expensive racing teams. One of the most successful riders of the era, Fiorenzo Magni (three times winner of the three-week Giro d'Italia, or Tour of Italy), said all the big bike companies in Italy, including Atala, Bianchi, Gloria and Legnano, were under terrible stress. The falling sales numbers for other European companies meant that all over Western Europe, bicycle and component makers faced severe financial hardship.

Magni's own sponsor, bike maker Ganna (started in 1910 by Luigi Ganna, winner of the first Giro d'Italia), told him they would not be able to fund his professional racing team in 1954. A creative and resourceful man, Magni turned to the German face cream company Nivea, which he knew about because racers put Nivea cream on the chamois lining of their cycling shorts. Nivea generously funded Magni's team, causing a huge uproar. The bicycle industry understood that if they lost their monopoly over team sponsorship and rich industrialists could enter the bidding, the bike companies would be priced out of the sport. Over the next three decades, that's what happened. But in the meantime, Magni had to fight with officials who wanted to forbid his wearing the Nivea jersey. He was castigated by the press, which was probably ignorant of the scale as well as the consequences of the bicycle market collapse. Besides, they didn't want money invested in racing by large non-cycling firms that could be more usefully spent, in their eyes, on print advertising.

The riders understood that Magni's move meant better paychecks for their profession. Fausto Coppi, the greatest champion of the era and an important draw to any race he entered, told the organizers of the important Paris–Roubaix race that if Magni couldn't wear his Nivea jersey, they would have to do without having Fausto Coppi in their race. Coppi's extortion won the day for Magni.

Even though there would be more difficulties for what are now called extra-sportif sponsors, the force of history was against the bike companies. Today, with but a few exceptions, bicycle makers supply bikes to teams

McGann

whose main sponsors are almost always outside the industry. Peugeot, whose racing sponsorship harkened back to the dawn of the twentieth century, financed its own high-end teams until 1986. They were one of the first in and were one of the last to give up. Another holdout, Raleigh, quit after the 1983 season.

Slowly, bicycle sales climbed, gaining about 10 percent between the mid-1950s and the mid-1960s. But that wonderfully fecund French imagination, that had tossed out bicycle innovations one after another, seemed to dry up. A 1966 Peugeot PX8 differed little (it had fenders and eight speeds) from the UO8 (no fenders and ten speeds) that the United Bicycle Sales staff was trying to change in 1973.

Simplex made one of the worst decisions ever in the history of the bicycle industry. Simplex began producing their fine deforming parallelogram Export 61 derailleur in 1961. With its sprung top pivot, it shifted better than the Campagnolo, it was that good. Then, with Peugeot paying for the engineering, incredibly Simplex began making this superb component out of polyoxymethylene plastic in 1962.

Simplex Prestige rear derailleur

Simplex and Peugeot hated people calling their derailleurs plastic. The proper term, they said, was "Delrin", a versatile thermoplastic Dupont began producing in 1961 that could be molded or machined.

In for a dime, in for a dollar. Simplex made the entire shifting ensemble, named Prestige, out of Delrin: shift levers, rear derailleur and front derailleur. To make matters worse, while the rest of the world moved to parallelogram front derailleurs that improve shifting by lifting the chain from the smaller

30

Why Your Bike Is Made in Asia

to the larger sprocket, Simplex stuck with its miserable, ancient pushrod design that simply shoved the chain back and forth. Good mechanics could bend the derailleur cages to get acceptable shifting from pushrod front derailleurs, but never anything like the more advanced parallelogram front changers from Campagnolo and Huret. Huret introduced its Allvit front parallelogram derailleur in 1961.

Simplex's short-sighted, cost-saving move using a largely untested raw material turned out to be a catastrophe. The levers broke, the springs of the rear derailleur came loose when the Delrin cracked and the balky front derailleurs were universally despised by mechanics. Simplex called the Delrin derailleur ensemble Prestige. They had none. They were junk. And yet Simplex persisted.

But, before crucifying Peugeot for failing to advance its bicycle (but then again perhaps we should leave them up on the cross for their part in Simplex's Delrin conversion), one has to remember that bicycle factories are first and foremost assemblers (defunct and now reborn Spanish parts and bike maker Zeus being a notable exception). Most, but not all, make their own frames (some simply buy frames) and build their bikes with components purchased from other makers. The UO8 was built with Simplex derailleurs, Solida cranksets, Normandy hubs, Atax bars and stems, Mafac brakes, Rigida rims, and so forth. At the factory Peugeot would build the wheels, mount the tires onto the wheels and perform the rest of the assembly. Peugeot was in no small part a slave of its suppliers. Starting in the mid-1950s, when so many bicycle and component makers failed, the vibrant competition that had fueled the steady stream of design advances largely ceased.

By the 1960s, as a result of the 1950s bicycle market collapse, each component niche was at best, an oligopoly; that is, a market with just a few surviving dominating players. For brakes, there was only Mafac or the less well-regarded CLB, unless a buyer wanted to source his product more expensively by going to Switzerland or Italy. By the mid-1960s there were only two French derailleur makers, Simplex and Huret (in 1950, there might have been as many as twenty); inexpensive hubs were made by Normandy. Steel cranksets were made by Nervar and Solida.

Consumer bikes are very price sensitive, and that sensitivity and long-standing business relationships that sometimes stretched back to the turn of the century kept French bicycle makers buying locally. With dozens of bicycle and component makers in or near St. Etienne (likewise with the Italian cycle industry centered in the north-east Veneto region), parts sourcing was little more than an exercise in local transportation.

Oligopolies are fairly common and whole forests have been felled to print studies of how they act. Since the bicycle industry and its consumers have been saddled with oligopolies and the consequences of their efforts to maximize profits, I hope the reader will forgive a short explanation of how a market might end up with just a few players and why they act the way they do.

The reason most often given for the emergence of an oligopoly is that a few companies in a market become very efficient producers. To take the French derailleur business, for example, both Huret and Simplex were able to ramp up their factories after the war and produce and sell thousands of derailleurs every week. They achieved what are called "economies of scale". They could buy their raw materials in huge lots, bringing down their costs. They could amortize their advertising over a larger number of derailleurs, and invest in manufacturing technology to make their factories more efficient and do longer production runs, which also reduce an item's unit cost.

Simplex and Huret both had substantial economies of scale and were the low-cost producers who could survive the fall in European bicycle sales in the 1950s.

Members of an oligopoly watch each other closely, wary of doing anything that might upset a profitable status quo. They must calculate how a rival will react to a move, a condition economists call "mutual interdependence". Studies have shown that if one member lowers his price to gain market share, it will be instantly matched. Wanting to avoid ruinous price wars, oligopolies rarely engage in price competition. They also tend to avoid another form of competition: technological improvement. This is understandable in light of their fear of an expensive technology war.

Even though they are generally in a superb financial position to invest heavily in product advancement, studies consistently show large firms in oligopolies are generally poor innovators. Analysis of patent statistics confirms that most technological advances come from small and mid-size firms or independent inventors. Economist Campbell McConnell wrote that an oligopolistic industry will produce less, provide fewer jobs and charge a higher product price than would the same industry if it were organized competitively.

Perhaps the most famous example of an oligopoly is the American automobile market of the 1950s and 1960s. GM, Ford and Chrysler made the same execrable cars year after year. Innovations were superficial. The famous Ford Mustang was just an old Ford Falcon with different sheet metal. The car makers were fat, profitable and content.

This outlook was shared by the 1960s French component makers. Simplex's move to Delrin can be understood in this light. Juy had his

Why Your Bike Is Made in Asia

customers. He could count on them for a steady stream of business, and he needed only to figure out how to reduce his costs to increase his profits.

The Huret Allvit parallelogram rear derailleur was introduced in 1958, almost a decade after Campagnolo introduced its deforming parallelogram derailleur. French cycling illustrator and writer Daniel Rebour wrote that by 1965, Huret had sold five million Allvit derailleurs. That year the firm was kicking out more than 100,000 Allvits a month! It was still on many bikes produced in 1974, sixteen years later.

There were flashes of competition, such as when Huret was willing to meet Simplex's lower price to get spec'd on the Schwinn Varsity. But

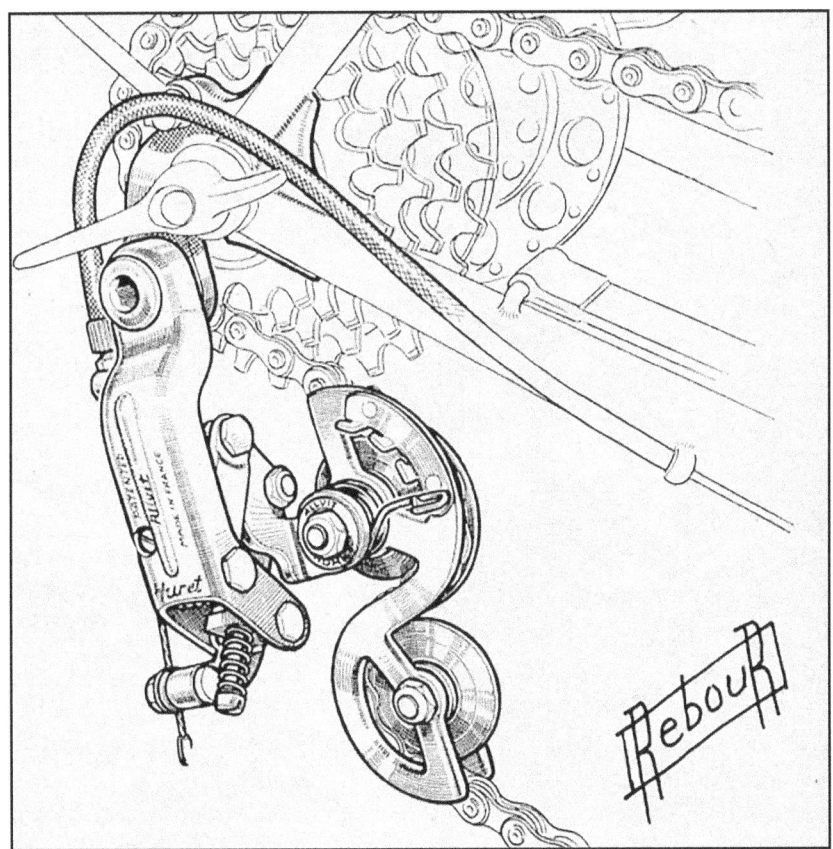

Daniel Rebour's drawing of the Huret Allvit rear derailleur, showing the parellelogram construction

in general, the French makers were behaving in a predictable way, not bothering to invest in their products because they didn't have to. One knowledgeable observer said that in addition to being mature companies, their managers were older men, hence conservative and resistant to innovation and preferring to keep everything in place.

French bicycle sales grew and production capacity expanded to meet the exploding demand of the 1970s. French makers were producing 900,000 bicycles a year in 1965. By 1974 they were making 2.4 million a year, of which 850,000 were exported, mostly to the United States. To meet this demand, Peugeot acquired a second factory. Yet, all was not well. To fill the orders pouring in, components were often substituted, paint quality was allowed to suffer and there were no thoughts of improving a hot-selling product. Daniel Rebour fretted over the fragility of low-end French bikes and how damaging their questionable quality might be in the long term to the reputation of the nation's cycle production and the overall health of the bicycle industry in France. His voice crying in the wilderness for improved French product was ignored.

In Great Britain, Raleigh was a giant amoeba, devouring brand after brand—including Carlton, BSA, Triumph, Gazelle (not to be confused with the Dutch Gazelle company, which made bikes for Raleigh in the 1970s) and Rudge—until there were few British competitors left who could produce any volume. By 1960 and now named TI-Raleigh, it was a behemoth employing 7,000 workers that had 75 percent of the British market. Raleigh had tried to compete with low-end American producers for the chain-store business, but gave up in the face of continual losses. Raleigh did penetrate the higher-end of the American market, having set up a warehouse and sales office in the U.S. that served 1,400 franchised dealers and sold 200,000 units a year in 1968. In the bike boom of the 1970s, that number grew to a half million.

Raleigh's growth was hard on the rest of the British cycle industry. Frank Berto wrote that because Raleigh was partially vertically integrated, making many of its own components (they owned Brooks Saddles, Sturmey-Archer hubs and Reynolds Tubing, among others), many British parts makers frozen out of Raleigh's production went out of business. In 1967 Raleigh decided to use Simplex derailleurs on its 10-speeds, probably sounding the death-knell for Cyclo's British derailleur factory, which stopped making changers in 1969. The Simplex derailleurs did no favors for Raleigh's reputation.

By June of 1974, European, and particularly French bicycle companies were busy, prosperous and content to sell their badly outdated product as long as they could. Like all successful businessman who find themselves rich because of fortunate circumstances they had nothing to do with (in this case, the bike boom), they counted themselves brilliant.

2
The boom hides the rot

In mid-1890s America, the safety bicycle's popularity created the first great bike boom, making bicycles one of America's major industries. Improbably, and showing the safety bicycle's enormous appeal, this great leap in sales was in the face of the Panic of 1893, probably America's worst depression until the 1930s.

At that time the largest bicycle company in the world was Colonel Albert Pope's Columbia, headquartered in Connecticut. Pope had acquired Pierre Lallement's original patent for the bicycle as well as every other patent pertaining to bicycles that he could buy. Pope had such a hammerlock on bicycle technology that all other American bicycle manufacturers had to pay him ten dollars a bike in licensing fees. Ten dollars then was far, far more money than it is today, an incredible $300.00 today's currency.

Though Pope displayed a robber-baron ferocity in the business world, he was a relentless promoter of the bicycle, fighting for improved roads and willing to pay the legal costs of riders caught up in laws passed to keep cyclists off some city streets. The horse-driven world of the late nineteenth century did not view the bicycle and its young, often heedless, speeding riders as an unmixed blessing. Called "Scorchers", aggressive, fast riders using bikes with poor brakes were vilified and feared by those who had to share the roads with them. Pope even personally paid to have one stretch of road paved. He was the fabled rising tide that lifts all boats.

Despite Columbia's success, the bikes that people rode in that 1890s bike boom were mostly produced around Chicago. For several decades in the nineteenth century Chicago was the world's fastest growing city, its easy water and rail transportation making it a perfect industrial hub. There, parts makers and bike assemblers sprang up in profusion, including the 1895 incorporation of Arnold, Schwinn & Company, the brainchild of German immigrant Ignaz Schwinn. Schwinn had worked for other factory owners, both in Germany and the U.S, but was always unhappy with the lack of control he felt his abilities warranted.

Financed by Adolf Frederick William Arnold, a prosperous meatpacker, Schwinn produced both his own bikes under the World brand, as well as private-label bikes for Sears and other retailers, adding his production to the more than one million bikes a year American factories were selling. Schwinn had two gifts, he was a superb promoter, able to give his bikes the publicity they needed in the crowded field of bike brands. And he was a conservative, careful businessman. When the inevitable business downturns happened, he could still turn a profit. The company said that under Ignaz Schwinn the firm never lost money.

Driven by the craze for the new safety bicycles, bikes were such a big business in the mid-1890s that an estimated 10 percent of American newspaper and magazine advertising was for bicycles and bicycle accessories. Even though everyone thought the boom years were just the new normal for the bicycle industry, sales began to slow in 1897, and by 1900, bike sales dropped to less than a quarter of what they had been five years before.

Sporting goods retailer and manufacturer A. G. Spalding tried to form a bicycle trust (with help from the greatest trust owner in history, John D. Rockefeller of Standard Oil), by getting the surviving manufacturers, notably Pope, who was desperate to save his business, to collude on price and production numbers. The bicycle industry has always been chaotic, filled with stubborn individualists like Schwinn and Iver Johnson, who refused to join. The trust found itself trying to herd cats and failed. Pope declared bankruptcy in 1907.

While the bicycle trust didn't gain traction, one important monopoly emerged from the wreckage of the trade's rescue efforts.

Pope had built his business on the high-wheeler and was a tardy convert to the safety bicycle. Safety bicycles required pneumatic tires rather than the solid hard-rubber band that was used on high-wheelers. Pope had no intention of licensing what Americans call clincher tires, which can easily be removed from the rim. Those designs were tied up in patents and Pope didn't pay licensing fees, he charged them. He looked around and saw the "single-tube tire", which at the time was unpatented.

In the single-tube tire, the tube is vulcanized to the tire to make a single unit. Justly called garden hose by its detractors, the single-tube tire was fragile and difficult to repair, but its technology looked to be free for the taking. Pope used single-tube tires on his bikes and encouraged other bike makers to do likewise.

Why Your Bike Is Made in Asia

Seeing his design succeed, single-tube tire inventor Pardon Tillinghast applied for and was granted a patent. Pope made the best of the situation and bought Tillinghast's patent, which stood up to an 1899 court challenge.

Out of the wreckage of Pope's business collapse, the Tillinghast patent changed hands a couple of times, ending up at the United States Rubber Company, which also owned the clincher tire and whatever might be left of the Dunlop rights in North America. U.S. Rubber (one of the original companies of the Dow Industrial Average, it later became Uniroyal, then Uniroyal-Goodrich) exploited its strength and bought out its competitors in the bicycle tire business. By 1911 it had a bicycle tire monopoly backed up with patents. And what U.S. Rubber wanted was to make and sell single-tube tires.

The bicycle industry acquiesced. There were understandable reasons for bicycle companies to use the single-tube tire. They were comparatively cheap, making the bike's retail price lower and more attractive. Mounted on wooden rims, the resulting bike was lighter. Because they were so difficult to repair, a cyclist had to buy new tires often. It seemed like a dream come true to U.S. Rubber.

Historian Paul Rubenson makes a compelling case that the single-tube tire scheme was a catastrophe. Because it rendered bicycles unreliable and costly to use, Americans refused to use them for general local transportation. Flat tires are what cyclists hate most, and American bikes with single-tube tires were not only prone to flats, the punctures were virtually irreparable. Moreover, because the single-tube tires were glued to wooden rims—which warped in damp weather—caliper brakes whose pads rubbed the sides of the rims were out of the question. This limited American bikes to either brakeless fixed gears (direct chain drive that made coasting impossible), brakes that rubbed the tire tread, or coaster brakes (pedal backwards to brake).

Bicycles became children's toys, no adult wanted to depend upon an American bike to get to work. Rubenson noted that American bicycle use collapsed and stayed at a very low level long before automobile ownership became common. In other words, contrary to the common assumption, cheap gas and Henry Ford's Model T were not the reasons Americans didn't take bicycles to heart. Americans had discarded the bike long before the Model T's price had dropped to an affordable $220 in the 1920s.

Another reason given for the failure of Americans to adopt the bicycle is the long distances and rural nature of most of the U.S. at the time. But other countries, even those with bad roads through rolling countryside like Italy, seized upon bicycles and developed important bike industries.

In Europe, bicycles became the most common form of transportation and bicycle sales steadily climbed. But the rest of the world wanted nothing to do with the single-tube tires Americans tried to export. They had practical wired-beaded tires that were simple to repair. Amsterdam of the 1930s had 400,000 bicycle commuters. A third of the adult population of Copenhagen traveled by bike. Certainly America had cities where tough, reliable bicycles would have been gratefully used.

Poverty forced my father to buy an old single-tube-tire bike in the 1930s. The misery those detestable tires caused him still rankled more than seventy-five years later. No wonder America preferred to walk or ride a horse. Even in depression-era America, cars outsold bicycles ten to one.

One can't help pondering what might have been. If American manufacturing genius had been applied to making more, better and cheaper bicycles, not just a few, more profitable bicycles, would the bicycle have become a part of American life as in Europe? Would mass-produced American bicycles have become dominant in the world market? Pope's seventeen-acre factory was a model of efficiency that gave him low production costs, and this was just at the birth of the industry. Would Frenchmen be racing the Tour of the United States? U.S. Rubber's imposition of the single-tube tire on the early twentieth-century American bicycle industry must go down as one of the greatest commercial misjudgments in U.S. history, one we pay for to this day.

All pictures of middle-aged Ignaz Schwinn show an unsmiling, serious face. His hair is neatly trimmed and there is a mustache that grew fuller

Ignaz Schwinn

Why Your Bike Is Made in Asia

over time. He became corpulent in old age and wore thick, wire-rimmed glasses. Born in Hardheim, Germany, Ignaz's father was a master carpenter. Ignaz spent much of his youth as an apprentice machinist. He fell in love with the new safety bicycle and as a young man began a partnership with a man named Henrick Kleyer to build the first safety bikes in Germany. The two fell out and their dispute is given as the reason Ignaz immigrated to America, ending up in Chicago.

He was a good manager whose conservative instincts served him well. When the bottom fell out of the 1890s bike business, his Arnold, Schwinn & Company still thrived. He even bought out a failed competitor (as well as partner Arnold) and set up a new, lower-cost factory. Before the First World War, Ignaz purchased a couple of motorcycle companies, notably Excelsior. In 1912 a Schwinn-made Excelsior was the first motorcycle to be officially clocked at more than 100 miles per hour. Schwinn did well selling high-end motorized two-wheelers until the onset of the great depression, which forced Schwinn to close its motorcycle factory.

Existing motorcycle production left the Schwinn family with just the bicycle business, which by 1930 had become a low-profit grind. Most American bikes were made for children and were sold through either mail-order firms like Sears, or chain stores. Looking to increase their profit margins, the parts makers arranged to sell their saddles, rims, spokes, etc. to the big retailers, but then had them drop-shipped directly to the bike factories. This deprived the bike maker of the profit of marking up the components' cost. The bike factory merely fabricated the frame and assembled the bike with parts owned by the customer. At the same time retailers pushed bike factories and parts makers to make ever cheaper, more poorly-made products, guaranteeing that bikes remained nothing more than children's playthings. The outlook of a business that had degenerated to the point that it didn't pay enough to maintain factory machinery was bleak.

Ignaz's son Frank W. Schwinn earned an engineering degree before joining the firm to work in the company's motorcycle division. As Ignaz aged, Frank W., a lean, bespectacled man, took on more responsibility. By the early 1930s he was running the entire firm, though Ignaz retained the title of president.

It's hard to overstate how difficult those early thirties were for Schwinn. Of the 194,000 bicycles sold in the U.S. in 1931, Schwinn historians Judith Crown and Glenn Coleman say that Schwinn sold only 17,000, and most of them highly discounted.

Frank W. fully comprehended the nature of the dead-end road he was on and decided to rebel. He would make high-quality bikes that would carry a good profit. He also knew the single-tube tire was preventing any large-scale success. He asked U.S. Rubber to make wired-on clincher tires and received the horselaugh in return. Frank went to Europe to learn more about the trade and came back with a stack of European-made clincher tires. He brought them to U.S Rubber. "Make tires or I'll import," he threatened.

Finally faced with competition, U.S. Rubber buckled and produced the 26 x 2.125 balloon tires with wire beads Schwinn needed. Schwinn then went to the other component makers and demanded parts made to his higher specifications. He re-designed the frame to allow clearances for the fatter tires. In 1933 Frank Schwinn introduced the Super Balloon Tire Bicycle to very dubious retailers and the public.

The Schwinn Super Balloon Tire Bicycle. Photo courtesy Gary Meneghin.

It was a smash hit. His plan to save his company by making a high-quality product turned out to be pure genius. He continued to improve his product and was rewarded by a marketplace that appreciated his departure from garbage. At $34.95 retail (an astonishing $800.00 in 2024 dollars), even though the country was in the depths of its greatest-ever depression, he was able to charge twice the going price for his bikes. From those 17,000 bikes sold in 1931, Schwinn's sales exploded to more than 100,000 in 1935.

Schwinn had no plans to transform how America traveled. He was interested in survival. Bikes were for kids, and kids' bikes he would

Why Your Bike Is Made in Asia

make. He would make them better, flashier, chromier and stronger than anyone else.

Almost immediately the entire bicycle industry abandoned the single-tube tire and within a year they had all but disappeared from new bike production. Sadly, it was too late to make the bicycle part of America's transportation DNA. But bicycles could now be trustworthy, low-cost transportation for kids.

From that 1933 revelation on, Frank W. Schwinn became a tyrant obsessed with quality and labored to make the Schwinn name synonymous with well-made bikes. He succeeded, his company's growing reputation for quality was well-deserved. Every boy who got a Sears or Montgomery Ward bike really wanted a Schwinn.

Confident in the quality of his bikes, instead of the industry standard one-year guarantee, in 1939 Frank W. began offering a lifetime guarantee on Schwinn frames and many of his bikes' parts.

By 1941, Schwinn was selling 346,000 bikes a year, twenty times what the firm had been selling in the early 1930s. Moreover, Schwinn had been innovating up a storm and over the decade the firm had been granted more than forty patents.

With other companies mimicking Schwinn's balloon-tired bike design, the entire industry's fortunes soared with bike production hitting numbers that hadn't been seen since the bike boom years of the late 1890s.

There was an important lesson. Frank W. had succeeded by making superb product that met his customers' desires. It was one that would have to be re-learned, over and over again. Even though Frank W. had set his firm on a course of higher profit margins, success in the bike manufacturing business still required a sharp pencil, which Frank W. used ruthlessly. Assembly workers could not count on year-round employment and when the yearly sales-season would slow in the winter, many were laid off and not brought back until April. And of course, like any Chicago factory, it was hot in the summer and cold in the winter, with fumes, dust and dirt everywhere.

Ignaz died in 1948 and left a time bomb that wouldn't go off for decades. His will created the Ignaz Schwinn Trust, which became Schwinn's sole stockholder. While the trust was financially generous to the family's female offspring, only the eldest male descendants held shareholder power. It was Ignaz's way to make sure the family retained control of the firm.

The year 1948 was important for Schwinn in another way. Schwinn stopped making private-label bikes for other firms. From that point on, Frank W., a man on a mission, intended to make and sell only Schwinns.

McGann

He succeeded admirably. As the post-war economic boom roared on, Schwinn made a quarter of the bikes sold in the U.S. in 1950. This was the largest market share Schwinn would ever capture, but according to Crown and Coleman, Schwinn's percentage of American market share during the 1950s would still impressively stay in the mid-teens. The depression and the specter of making bikes that could not be sold for their manufacturing cost was truly in the rear-view mirror. The estimated $25 million a year in business Schwinn was doing in the mid-1950s converts to roughly $280 million in 2024 dollars. This was a real business.

The company's success was well-deserved. Frank W. was a man devoted to making the finest, highest-quality bicycle possible and he succeeded. The Schwinn bikes of the 1950s were superbly made. Again, the intention was to make bikes that would warm the hearts of children and teenagers, and stand up to the torture kids give bikes. They were bikes worthy of the Schwinn Lifetime Guarantee.

After the war's end in 1945, as part of his continuing efforts to strengthen Schwinn, Frank W. now targeted his retailers. Up to that point, Schwinns were sold through a hodge-podge of thousands of stores, many of which weren't bicycle shops at all, and only some were capable of competently assembling or repairing a bike. Among the 15,000 retailers offering Schwinns were not only grungy bike shops, but pool halls, barber shops and gas stations. For a man wanting to sell $80.00 kids' bikes (even as late as 1960, adjusting for inflation an $80.00 Schwinn becomes an $800.00 bike in 2024 dollars) the early 1950s retail bike outlets were far from Frank W.'s vision of the way to sell his bikes.

Knowing that a dumpy store or incompetent mechanic could be just as destructive to a customer's perception of Schwinn's quality as a bad paint job, Frank W. set about cutting its dealer list and forbidding its distributors from selling to unapproved retailers.

Frank W.'s right hand man Ray Burch (who eventually had the title of senior vice-president of marketing) had a couple of bike shops in mind that he thought his Schwinn dealers should emulate as they were pushed and prodded into modernizing their outlets. Helen Throckmorton's family had retailed bicycles in Santa Monica, California, since the mid-1930s. She hated the very idea of the crummy, dirty shop selling bikes and finally, in the early 1960s, had an architect design a big, open store building with giant windows for "Helen's Cycles". Burch wanted his dealers to copy Helen's and give their Schwinn bikes a modern, well-lit, spacious setting. He really wanted them to do nothing more than be like other good retailers of nearly every other product.

Why Your Bike Is Made in Asia

The other shop was George Garner's Schwinn shop in Panorama City, also in southern California. Garner was so outspoken about both other dealers' and Schwinn's shortcomings that Schwinn eventually talked him into moving to Northbrook, a city close to Chicago so that Schwinn could show dealers traveling to Schwinn's headquarters in Chicago what a shop should look like. In fact, those who embraced Burch's vision (at no small cost) were generally rewarded with sharply increased sales that made the remodeling well worthwhile. Crown and Coleman noted that as result of Schwinn's efforts to bring its retailers into the mid-twentieth century, the number of dealers selling 1,000 or more Schwinn bikes in a year jumped from 48 in 1963 to 455 in 1968.

Schwinn's two-pronged marketing was very forward-looking. The company not only advertised in *Boy's Life*, the magazine put out by the Boy Scouts of America, Schwinn also had TV personality Captain Kangaroo endorse Schwinns on his morning show for children. This is where Schwinn's forward-looking vision really shows. The TV show was for very young children, just about ready for a bike. But Schwinn was working on the next demographic cohort to want a Schwinn.

The other effort was to improve the dealer. It began with one Schwinn employee who gave assistance to dealers visiting Schwinn's headquarters, answering their repair questions. Schwinn's efforts to turn its dealers into skilled, capable mechanics was realized when Schwinn began a dealers' school. Plus Schwinn worked to teach its dealers the basics of business finances. It was all geared to make a Schwinn shop beautiful, spacious, well-lit and owned by a capable, skilled retailer who made money. It worked. Good bikes offered from a good store made Schwinn the bike people wanted, starting from before they entered school and then on into adulthood.

Afraid of transgressing anti-trust laws, the firm performed its due diligence, going so far as to having a meeting with a staff member of the Federal Trade Commission. Schwinn was told they could proceed to cut off dealers if they had guidelines that were publicly accessible, were followed fairly and enforced without favoritism. Schwinn then went about cutting its dealer network in half.

Despite its attempt to avoid trouble with the government, Schwinn did end up earning the wrath of the U.S. Department of Justice, which saw this move as a violation of federal anti-trust laws. In 1957 the government filed a lawsuit against Schwinn that would grind through the legal system for a decade before finally arriving at the U.S. Supreme Court. Most of what Schwinn had done to control its retail outlets was ruled legal, but

McGann

the Supreme Court held Schwinn could not control where distributors sold Schwinn bikes. Once a distributor bought a Schwinn product, the Schwinn company no longer had control of the product. The lawsuit cost Schwinn a million 1967 dollars (about $8 million in 2024 dollars) and was an enormous drain on the company's energy and resources.

Schwinn had a ready response to the 1967 decision. They severed relationships with their distributors and spent millions setting up their own warehouses all over the country. It was another huge expenditure of money, energy and time for the mid-size company.

In 1963 Frank W. Schwinn passed control of the firm to his oldest son, Frank Valentine Schwinn. That same year Frank W. died of prostate cancer.

Frank V. didn't have his father's or grandfather's passion for manufacturing. He was more attracted to finance, distribution and marketing. An introverted man with a slight stutter, he had attended a military academy before going on to college and then serving in the U.S. Army Air Corps as an officer during World War II.

By the late 1960s, with the financial stresses of the lawsuit and the new distribution channels being set up, men and women working in the Schwinn factory (managed by Frank V.'s brother, Edward) began to notice the machinery was wearing out and not being replaced, even though the marketing department was swimming in money. The core reason for Schwinn's success was its devotion to making the best bikes in the country and that was being forgotten. Still, despite the rickety manufacturing plant, the Schwinn trust kicked out a million dollars a year in dividends to the family, give or take a couple hundred thousand.

Schwinn wasn't the only company making bikes in the U.S., not by a long shot. In the 1950s Frank W. had finished the long-term job of pulling Schwinn out of the chain-store and mail-order business. But there were other makers, all in the Midwest, happy to take the big retailers' money.

Huffy bicycles harken back to the nineteenth century. George P. Huffman acquired the Davis Sewing Machine Company in 1887 and moved the factory from Watertown, New York to Dayton, Ohio. By 1892 Huffman was making bicycles. His son Horace started his own firm, the Huffman Manufacturing Company in 1924, which in the beginning made equipment for gasoline service stations and steel bicycle rims. When the depression hit, Horace decided to go into the bike business, feeling the lower-cost transportation mode would be attractive in hard times. The company made bikes branded Dayton, initially twelve bikes a day but within two years the company was kicking out 200 bikes a day. But this was not enough for Huffman's main customer, Firestone tire stores, and in 1938,

Why Your Bike Is Made in Asia

Huffman lost a lot of Firestone's business because he could not fill the tire company's orders.

Huffman built an ultra-modern conveyerized assembly-line that by 1940 had doubled production. With this increased production capability, the company was able to regain Firestone's business and acquire more customers, including the (now long gone) Western Auto chain with its 5,200 locations. Though Huffman had tried to sell higher-quality bikes, moving up-market and getting rid of a cheap-product image is one of the hardest challenges in marketing. Huffman gave up and stuck to doing what it had been doing, making low-cost bikes.

After the war, Huffman and his bicycles went from strength to strength, growing as the company became an important supplier to mass-merchant retail chains. In 1949 the company produced its first Huffy bicycle, the Huffy Convertible. It was a 20-inch wheel bike that looked like 26-inch bikes, with a sheet-metal "gas tank" that covered the top tube. It was the first bike with training wheels with footsteps so that a second child could stand behind the rider.

In 1953 the firm began branding all of its bicycles Huffy. The firm kept expanding its bike offerings. Perhaps its most surprising bike was 1955's "RadioBike". The firm installed a radio in the bike's top-tube tank and a battery pack on the rear carrier. Though transistor radios had long been available—the American-made Regency TR-1 since Christmas of 1953 and Sony's mass-market TR-63 portable radio since 1957—Huffy's bike radio had fragile vacuum tubes. A transistor radio cost about $40.00 then, not much less than the complete RadioBike, hence the vacuum tube radio. Huffy sold the bike for three years.

In the first years of the 1960s, boys began customizing their 20-inch bikes with high-rise handlebars and long "banana" seats supported in the back with a sissy bar that came above the back of the seat, mimicking chopper motorcycles. Southern California bicycle distributor John T. Bill contacted Huffy and asked the firm to make "Chopper" twenty-inch bikes. Though hesitant, Huffy agreed if John T. Bill would buy all the special parts that Huffy would have acquire to make the choppers if the bike didn't sell.

John T. Bill agreed and the first banana-seat bicycle, called The Penguin, went on sale in 1963. Through the sixties the bike, now called the Rail, grew ever fancier, with steering wheels and top-tube mounted stick shift lever to change gears. Yes, the bikes could come with derailleurs. The steering wheel and stick shift were removed when the U.S. Government's Consumer Protection Safety Commission mandated that they be discontinued.

McGann

By 1973 Huffman had five factories, 2,500 employees and was publicly traded on the American Stock Exchange. No bike mechanic of the 1970s will ever forget the mustard-yellow and brown $79.99 Huffy Scout. People bringing a Scout to a bike shop for repair were generally advised to throw the bike away and buy a new one. But price was what drove Huffy's sales and by 1976 it was America's best-selling brand.

Murray Ohio Manufacturing Company started making automobile parts when it opened its factory in Cleveland in 1919. By the mid-1930s the company was making bicycles for the youth market. Murray joined the fight for department and chain-store business, making bikes for Western Auto, Sears and Firestone. Looking to reduce costs and avoid labor unions, Murray moved to Tennessee in the 1950s, but the United Auto Workers found them anyway and unionized the plant. Bike shop mechanics may not have fond memories of Murray bikes, but in the 1970s it was a giant enterprise, its factory floor covered forty-two acres. Most Americans wanted cheap bikes, mainly for their kids, and Murray made them.

There were others. AMF (an industrial conglomerate that also produced nuclear reactors and inter-continental ballistic missile silos) made Roadmaster bicycles in Olney, Ohio. Despite its imposing name, the 1970s Roadmaster may represent the nadir of American cycle manufacturing.

There was a standout among the other American bike makers, Ross Bicycles. In the 1980s the New York bike maker was the third-largest producer of bicycles in the U.S., behind Schwinn and Huffy. The firm was started in 1940 as the Ross Galvanizing Works to make pipes and pipe fittings for the fencing industry and then during the war galvanized steel parts for military ships.

In 1946 the company changed its name to Chain Bike Corp and began making bikes at its Williamsburg, New York factory under the helm of Sherwood Ross, son of company founder Albert Ross. In 1973 the firm moved to a purpose-built bike factory in Allentown, Pennsylvania. Unlike the other non-Schwinn bike makers, Ross made decent bikes, suitable for bike shop sales. And they were repaid for their fine product, selling a million bicycles a year by the late 1960s. In their home market of New York, Ross outsold Schwinn.

I still remember a visit to my shop in what must have been the late 1970s by company vice-president Randy Ross and a Ross salesman on what I assume was a sales trip looking to open up West Coast dealers. They showed me their bike, which was quite good. But by then I was selling flawless Japanese Centurion bikes and preferred their still-higher quality.

Why Your Bike Is Made in Asia

Not wanting to upset or insult the two gentlemen, I demurred on explaining why I didn't want to sell what was, indeed, a fine American-made bike. But they pressed me and I said that I thought the Ross bikes weren't quite as good as the Centurions. Randy Ross got really angry with me, insulted that I had denigrated the bikes that his firm had worked so hard to make first-rate.

Ross was attuned to the market and in 1982 the company was one of the first to mass-produce a mountain bike and even had its own factory racing team. That year the company changed its name to Ross Bicycles.

Despite its heavy investment in its bike factory, looking to keep its costs under control, Ross moved its bike production to Taiwan in 1986.

While Randy was working on keep the bicycle business profitable, Sherwood Ross was working on government supply contracts, notably ammunition boxes. The company lost so much money making product for the government that Ross filed for bankruptcy in 1986. The Ross brand was purchased in 1988 by Rand International, which turned the brand into a department store bike.

Early in 1963 over in Chicago, Schwinn executive Al Fritz was made aware of the chopper bikes and began working on a Schwinn version. Southern California dealers knew this was what boys wanted. The Southern California Schwinn distributor knew of his dealers' need for chopper bikes

A 1963 ad for the
Schwinn Sting-Ray

and promised Fritz an opening order of 500. Upon seeing a prototype of the odd bike with a banana seat, high-rise bars and fat tires, Frank V. was dubious, but Fritz was insistent.

Fritz was right. Really, really right. The bike was available for sale in the second half of 1963 and Schwinn sold 45,000 Sting-Rays that year with dealers begging for more. The hold-up was getting enough of the special fat tires that helped give the bike its distinctive look. Between 1963 and 1968 Schwinn sold almost two million Sting-Ray bikes.

Understandably, soon Murray, AMF and Columbia were making their own versions of the Sting-Ray.

By the late 1960s Sting-Ray sales slowed. But, Schwinn was ready. The company had another bike ready that was brilliantly designed for older boys, the Varsity. Through the 1950s the Schwinn Varsity was an upright three-speed bike. In 1960 the Varsity was transformed into a drop-bar, eight-speed derailleur bike with 26-inch tires, welded mild-steel frame and one-piece steel cranks. Rugged and heavy-duty, it was perfect for a boy to use to go explore his world. That 1960 model came with a Simplex 15D pull-chain rear derailleur and a Simplex front derailleur whose pivot was mounted on a seat-tube braze-on. The rider would reach down and move the lever to change the front gears while pedaling.

A big improvement came in 1962 when it became a 10-speed with Huret parallelogram derailleurs. The derailleurs not only shifted much better, the rear derailleur was far more rugged. Both the front and rear derailleurs could now be used by pulling on downtube-mounted levers. The next year the Varsity was given 27-inch wheels.

Schwinn had hit another home run. Crown and Coleman wrote that in the early 1970s Schwinn was kicking out 400,000 Varsitys a year and was making 80 percent of the derailleur-equipped bikes produced in the United States. This was true market dominance, the result of Schwinn's making durable, well-made bikes that Americans had come to love. I remember the contempt the other kids in junior high had for my quite nice Sears bike made by Austrian maker Steyr-Puch with its Fiamme aluminum rims, AVA aluminum bars and stem and light-weight lugged frame. It could have been made of titanium, but since it did not have a Schwinn badge, it drew contempt and derision from the other kids.

Indicative of the company's success, in the late 1960s and early 1970s, the Schwinn trust was still disbursing about a million dollars a year to the Schwinn family, give or take a couple hundred thousand dollars. Life was good when you were a Schwinn.

3
Asian suppliers get a foothold

The merciless, completely price-oriented business of supplying chain stores gave Japanese component makers their first real opening into the American bike market. After Raleigh of England decided to stop chasing the private-label chain-store bike business, Western Auto found itself without a supplier for its Western Flyer bicycles. There was time when Western Auto was a big deal, with 1,200 company-owned stores and more than 4,000 privately owned franchised shops. Desperate, Western Auto turned to Columbia, which, through a complex series of sales and mergers, was the financial descendant of Pope's company. Western Auto gave Columbia an order for 175,000 three-speed bikes. Raleigh owned Sturmey-Archer, the maker of the three-speed hub Americans had always used. But Raleigh demanded a price for the highly-respected hubs that rendered the Columbia bikes too expensive for Western Auto. This was trouble because the bike's retail price was locked in, Western Auto had already printed its catalogue.

The only solution available to Columbia was to use the less-expensive and not-quite-as-well-made Shimano three-speed hub, which had been produced since 1957. After some fussing over putting Japanese parts on Western Auto bikes, the desperate buyers acquiesced and in 1963, what was I believe the first major OEM (original equipment manufacturer) purchase of Japanese bicycle parts by an American bike maker was consummated. It was a seminal transaction. Other low-end makers quickly jumped on the low-cost Japanese parts bandwagon and soon Japan was exporting $100 million a year worth of bike parts to the U.S.

Americans had been buying bikes in ever greater numbers in the 1960s, but then it was mostly a kids' bike market. Of the bicycles sold in the mid-1960s, 95 percent were for children. Sometime in 1970, for reasons that are still being debated, people started buying more bicycles, and not just children's bikes as in the past. Adults wanted to start riding.

In 1960, total American bicycle sales were 3.7 million units, 5.6 million in 1965 and 6.9 million in 1970. Sales jumped to 8.9 million in 1971 and then incredibly, Americans bought 13.9 million bikes in 1972. For the first time in decades, more bikes than cars were sold in the U.S. and half of them were for adults and 37 percent of these bikes were imported. But the arc was still aimed skyward when 1973's sales topped 15.2 million. In 1974 the air began to come out of the boom's tires when sales fell to 14.1 million.

In 1975, Crash! 7.3 million bikes were sold in the U.S., not far from 1970's volume.

What caused this boom? Some sociologists point to the growing counter-culture, Earth Day, Volkswagen Beetles and a general disaffection with big Detroit iron as well as America's overall prosperity. This is overthinking the question. Bikes, especially 10-speed bikes, were a popular fad (even if clothed in a socially conscious wrapping) in the early 1970s. Owning a Motobecane imported from France was fashionable, like a hula hoop in the late 1950s. People would brag about their Peugeots and boast that their Raleighs had center-pull brakes.

Events on the other side of the world prolonged the bike boom. During the three-week Arab-Israeli war in October, 1973, (also known as the Yom Kippur War) the United States was one of the few countries to side with Israel, while the Soviet Union supported Egypt and Syria. Saudi Arabia responded by promising to reduce oil production 5 percent a month.

On October 19, President Nixon authorized more than $2 billion in military aid to Israel. The Organization of Arab Petroleum Exporting Countries response was a complete oil embargo targeting the United States, Canada, Japan, South Africa and several European countries.

The price of oil in the United States quickly quadrupled, going from three to twelve dollars a barrel. The problem was exacerbated by ham-fisted oil price-controls imposed by the Nixon administration. As early as 1972 rationing resulting from the price controls began causing lines at gas stations. By late 1973, buying gas had become a real problem. Anyone who drove a car then remembers odd and even days, when one's license plate number determined when one could buy gas.

This gave bike sales an extra boost when they might have collapsed earlier. People were desperately looking for an alternative to their cars and continued flocking to bike shops. The embargo was lifted in March, 1974 and overnight America resumed driving. But oil would never again be the insanely cheap commodity it had been.

All fads and fashions have limited lives, even though they can seem at the time to be a permanent change, and the great bike boom of the

Why Your Bike Is Made in Asia

1970s was no exception. The bike boom's end was no doubt accelerated by the great bear market of 1973 and 1974, when the stock market lost 45 percent of its value and the brutal slowdown of the American economy left Americans feeling poor.

The boom had transformed the entire landscape of the bicycle industry. In 1971 Schwinn sold out its entire year's production in May and put the dealers on allocation until 1974. Ominously, in an effort to meet the extraordinary demand from a factory already suffering from deferred maintenance, Schwinn's legendary quality (already under stress because of the deteriorating production machinery) suffered. Wheels were badly built (old dealers still gripe about the inspection approval tags on Schwinn Varsitys with bent wheels) and the paint was often poor as the factory ran three shifts. Still, Schwinn couldn't meet the incredible demand for its bikes. In most towns, the Schwinn dealer was the most respected and highest volume bike shop. In their efforts to create an elite corps of retailers, the Schwinn family had succeeded admirably.

For years Schwinn had been working to make the Schwinn dealers' showrooms 100 percent Schwinn with no competing product to mar the "Schwinn Concept" retail model. Many had done so. But now, not wanting to miss out on the business of a lifetime and Schwinn unable to fulfill its orders, its dealers turned to imported bikes. Even more importantly, starting in 1972, Schwinn itself imported Japanese bikes in an effort to both sate their dealers' demand for enough bikes and supply a lugged road bike lighter than the thirty-eight-pound Continental. The company was careful. These first bikes were not branded Schwinn. Instead, harkening back to Schwinn's earliest days, they were World-brand bikes and did not even appear in the Schwinn catalogue. After the initial shipments, they were given "Schwinn Approved" decals.

Despite these efforts, by selling bikes made by Panasonic and Bridgestone, Schwinn was saying, in effect, the magic of the made-in-Chicago Schwinn quality didn't really exist. Bike shops not selling Schwinn seized on this lever to promote their own brands.

In late 1973, feeling a growing softness in the business, a few Schwinn dealers cancelled some of their orders. At the height of the 1974 season with gas rationing a thing of the past, the order cancellations became a flood. The boom for Schwinn and the rest of the industry was over.

4
Howie ignites the tinder

Howie Cohen was a big, avuncular bear of a man whose ready smile and friendly, disarming disposition hid a penetrating intellect and an adamantine determination. His father, Leo J. Cohen, Sr. started selling bikes in Minneapolis as part owner of the family-run Cycle Goods Company in 1939, the year Howie was born. He grew up surrounded by bicycles.

Howie Cohen

After the war, the Cohens sold back their share of the business and moved to Los Angeles, where they bought Atlas Cycle and renamed it Playrite Bicycle Supply Company. In those post-war years the Cohens did a huge business restoring used bicycles. Rebuilding old bikes meant re-spoking damaged wheels, matching factory paint, including Schwinn's

McGann

pinstriping and two-tone paint jobs, as well as doing everything else needed to make an old bike new again. Howie learned to do it all and gained a deep knowledge of bicycles and the bike trade.

The Cohens' business grew to restoring 2,000 bikes a year. They began buying their tires and tubes directly from the factories like Pennsylvania Rubber and Carlisle rather than from wholesalers. In those days of balloon-tired bikes, nearly every bike restoration called for a new set of fenders, which they bought directly from McCauley (fender supplier to Schwinn) and Elrae. Nearby shops started buying parts from Playrite.

Howie recalled, "Dad, who was president of the Southern California Bicycle Association, asked some of the other dealers who were active in the association if they would like to get in on a better deal than buying from a wholesaler." With his successful retail operation covering his overhead, Cohen could undercut the wholesalers' price.

"Then, another big step for us happened about 1956 when the Harry Wilson Sales Agency, the distributor for the Whizzer Motor Company [Ed. note: also the Southern California and Arizona Schwinn distributor], which made motors for bicycles, wanted to give it up and asked Dad if he would take it over. We did take it over and became the distributor for the eleven western states. That gave us the intro to sell other bicycle parts to those dealers we were selling Whizzer to."

The distribution side gradually took over, prompting the Cohens to launch a wholesale company, West Coast Cycle. By 1957, one Playrite shop had been liquidated and the building torn down to make a parking lot, and the other shop was sold. The Cohens had become dedicated bicycle wholesalers.

In 1958, they bought a 30,000 square-foot three-story building in Los Angeles for their warehouse. Leo Sr. started buying bikes from other distributors such as Les Engel, who was importing Girardengo bicycles from Italy, and George Joannou in New York who brought in Dunelt (Raleigh later acquired Dunelt). Engle and Joannou acted as sales agents for their brands, allowing West Coast Cycle to receive its bikes directly from the European factories. At first the bikes were brought in by the dozen and as West Coast Cycle grew, the orders swelled to hundreds at a time.

In about 1960 Leo Sr. traveled to the Earl's Court bicycle show in London. He made contact with Falcon and Elswick-Hopper (which may have been sharing its factory with Falcon by this time) and contracted to import their bikes directly.

Having a good eye for interesting product as well as knowing what his customers would like, Leo Sr. also ordered 100 replicas of the highwheeler

Why Your Bike Is Made in Asia

bikes Falcon had custom fabricated to bring attention to their London show booth. Some of Leo's high-wheelers are still in use today. The following year Leo Sr. returned to Earl's Court and made a deal with Raleigh to import two brands Raleigh owned and produced, Royal Scot and Meteor (the better of the two).

West Coast Cycle was now a major player in the bike wholesale business, importing two and three thousand bikes at a crack: 3-speeds and 10-speeds, 26- and 27-inch-wheeled bikes from Raleigh and 27-inch racing bikes from Falcon. This was before containerized shipping had become widely adopted.

When Leo Sr. was bringing in his Meteors, bicycles were "break-bulk" cargo, each bike was delivered partially assembled in its own heavy cardboard box as loose freight to a warehouse at the harbor. The bikes (or toasters, car bumpers, alarms clocks and any other freight that wasn't delivered in bulk, like coal or grain) were placed on large pallets and delivered by crane into the steamship's storage holds. The bikes were hand-stacked, six or seven tiers high by stevedores, who had to walk on the cargo to do their job, leaving their foot-prints on the boxes. They also left bent fenders and crushed boxes in their wake. Howie was philosophical, "That's the way it was done in those days."

"And they would off-load them the same way. Stand on the bikes and load them onto pallets attached to a cable. The crane would pull them out of the hold and land them on a flat-bed truck, where the trucker would take them off the pallet and hand-stack them back on the truck. They would drive down to our place, where we would off-load them. The driver would hand them to me, my brother (Leo Jr.) and other employees, and we would stack them on pallets, sorting out the models and colors, and then send them up our freight elevator, one pallet at a time with nine bicycles on it. With a shipment of 3,000 bikes, there would be truck after truck coming up from the harbor because they could only load about 200 bicycles on a flatbed truck."

Break-bulk international bike transport was slow, expensive, labor-intensive and fraught with rampant theft. It made each parcel a likely recipient of some form of shipping damage.

Soon "unitized" break-bulk shipping became available, where fourteen or sixteen bikes were attached to a pallet secured with metal bands at the factory and delivered that way to the consignee. This drastically reduced the individual handling each bike had received and meant the shipments arrived in far better condition, with far fewer dents and scratches. But it was still a long way from what Howie thought acceptable.

McGann

Unitized shipping was a short-lived solution because around 1963 containerized ocean freight became almost universal. An empty steel box about eight feet tall and eight feet wide and either twenty or forty feet long would be delivered to a factory. It would be loaded and sealed by the shipper and could be put on a standardized truck bed and delivered to a purpose-built ship (a modern Ultra Large Container Vessel in 2024 can carry more than 24,000 containers). At the destination dock, the container would then be loaded onto either a freight car or a truck before arriving at its destination. Only then the seal was broken and the container opened. Costs, damage and theft plummeted.

In December of 1963, Leo Sr. passed away, but the family pressed on in the bicycle wholesale business. By this point Howie was beside himself over the problems they were having with defects and shipping damage. His anguish was shared by dealers who would come to the warehouse with bikes fresh out of the box with bent fenders or scratched frames. There were other quality-control problems as well, such as filings and sawdust in the crankset bearings and paint that didn't stick to the bikes (problems 1970s bike boom mechanics would recognize). He would have to give the dealer a new bike and then repair the returned bike and sell it at a discount. West Coast set up a small shop in the warehouse with a workman who used to work at Playrite restoring used bikes. The defect rate was so large, his sole job was fixing returned bikes.

In early 1964, Howie's mother, RosaBelle, sent him to England to see if Falcon and Raleigh could be talked into improving their quality and packing.

Howie was emphatic. None of these problems required a difficult solution. There was nothing that could not be fixed if someone cared to fix it. But for reasons that always escaped Howie, the British makers were simply uninterested in changing. "There was no sense of urgency on their part. But remember, I was a very young man, just twenty-three, with very little patience and thought I knew everything." He believed he was bringing a punch list of easy-to-solve problems that should never have been allowed to get in the way of building a business based on quality product and service.

After three weeks of "terrific dinners and meeting some really nice people" but getting absolutely no satisfaction to his requests, he returned home. His conclusion when he reported to RosaBelle was grim. "We should sell the company and do something else." He didn't see a future for the family in the bicycle import business with the way things were heading. In addition to the quality control problems, importing Raleigh-made bikes didn't pencil.

Why Your Bike Is Made in Asia

"Because Raleigh distributed their own bikes in the U.S., we were competing with our supplier. In order for them to sell their bikes here, they had to set reasonable price points. In order for us to sell our bikes, we had to have our price points in line with theirs. They controlled our costs, and they controlled our selling price. We had no control over our margins."

Since 1962, Kazuo Takai of the Japan Bicycle Promotion Institute (he was also working for Shimano) had been calling on RosaBelle, telling her Japanese companies could make good bicycles that West Coast Cycle should try.

Not one to give up without a fight, RosaBelle told Howie to go to Japan and meet with Mr. Takai and see the factories there. This was well before faxes and even before Telex machines were common. Shortly after Howie's return from England, a Western Union cablegram was sent to Takai telling him that Howie would like to meet him in Japan and visit factories interested in producing quality bicycles. Howie added that he wanted to see Japanese bicycles that were different from what he had so far seen exported to America.

The bicycles Japan was sending to the U.S. were like nearly everything that came from Japan in the immediate post-war years. They were garbage. At the time independent bike dealers did not sell Japanese bicycles. Companies like Royce Union (then the biggest buyer of Japanese bikes) specialized in supplying department stores, where price was the only consideration. Importers had hammered the Japanese into producing 3-speed bikes that retailed for $19.95. Equipped with whitewall tires, chrome fenders and 3-speed gears, some even had a generator and light set.

To keep the prices low, the bikes usually went directly from the Japanese factory to the department store warehouse and were never touched by the importer. Howie says he never learned what the Japanese were charging for their department store bikes, but given what he knew about freight and necessary markups, he guesses that it was around ten dollars. It must be remembered that ten 1964 dollars was a lot more money than it is today, my 1964 Chevrolet Bel Air cost around $2,500. The Japanese wanted the American bike business and the $10 bike was the purchase order on the table. For the moment they accepted the terms of the low-profit transaction.

Howie's vision was revolutionary. He craved a bike that did not exist, a synthesis of the best of American and European bikes. He wanted the bullet-proof reliability and high quality of a 1960 Schwinn built into a fun, good-riding, lightweight Euro bike and he wanted it to sell for no more than other bikes then sold in bike shops. It hardly seems like a huge leap today, but then it was a breathtaking ambition. It's no wonder he doubted that his trip to Japan would be any more successful than his voyage to Britain.

Car buyers were in many ways victims of the same complacent business culture that was driving Howie mad. At 40,000 miles, my own 1964 Chevrolet burned oil and the crank journals had worn oblong. The body rusted even though I lived in coastal southern California where there is less rainfall than in Beirut. Owners of European import cars were usually no better off. MGs leaked oil and Peugeots were difficult to start. America was the wealthiest country in the world at the peak of its power. But everyone was buying disposable junk from an industrial culture than enshrined planned obsolescence.

Takai sent Howie a telegram welcoming him with open arms. In the spring of 1964 Howie flew to Japan. 1964 was an important year in post-war Japanese history. Tokyo hosted the summer Olympic Games, a way to show the world that Japan was now part of the First World. Even more telling, Tokyo erected its first skyscraper, the New Otani Hotel, overcoming the severe challenges high-rise construction presents in seismically active areas. Japan was by then remarkably advanced in many areas, including steel, cameras, shipping and electronics. But the mighty Japanese industrial engine which would become "Death, The Destroyer of Worlds" that turned vast swaths of the American industrial landscape into rusty, abandoned factories was still more than a decade away.

Howie spent about a month in Japan, visiting two to four factories a day. Either Shimano or the Japanese Bicycle Promotion Institute (Howie isn't sure) provided a car and a driver. Howie was in a completely new world and depended upon Takai to handle everything. He had no idea where he was being driven and couldn't even pronounce the names of the people he met.

But for all the courtesy and earnestness Howie encountered in his hosts, he was discouraged. "They were all making junk. Not only were the frames junk, the components were junk. The poor bikes didn't have a chance. Once something went wrong, everything went wrong."

When asked if the Japanese bikes were comparable to those that Murray was producing, Howie put the dreadful Japanese production he was inspecting in context, "No, they [Murray bikes] were much better bikes, much, much better, with really strong frames. The chrome was a little more decent than the Japanese chrome."

After visiting perhaps a hundred bicycle factories, Howie found nothing he could buy. They had all said they could make high-quality bicycles, but nothing in a month of traveling in Japan had made Howie believe this was

Why Your Bike Is Made in Asia

even remotely true. Part of it was a difference in a basic understanding of what a good bike was. Howie had one idea of what that meant and he was sure the Japanese view was something else.

Howie flew home and reported to RosaBelle. "There isn't a factory over there we can deal with."

"Did you see ALL the factories in Japan?"

"No."

"If you didn't, go back and see the others."

Six weeks later he went back to Japan.

Again, he visited factory after factory. After three weeks of relentless searching, he still couldn't find a maker that could build his bikes. On the day before he was scheduled to fly home, he got a call from a trading company called Maruka Machinery. Maruka explained they knew he was looking for high-quality bicycles and said there was a factory named Kawamura in Kobe that could make them. Howie asked Takai if he knew about Kawamura and Takai said they were a good outfit.

Underlining the seething ambition driving 1960 Japanese industrialists, that day a paid-for airplane ticket was delivered to Howie's hotel. At 5 AM the next morning he flew from Tokyo to Osaka where he was met by Takai and the Maruka people, who drove him to the factory, an hour away.

Howie toured the Kawamura plant and met its management. He was surprised by what he found. Kawamura was a very serious company that seemed capable of making what Howie wanted. He was particularly impressed by the president of the company, Yukio Kawamura, and "his sincerity and his desire to get away from Royce Union and Western Auto type bikes, which he was doing for his survival, not because it was what he wanted to do."

Things went well enough that Howie and about twenty Kawamura staffers had a sumptuous lunch at the Oriental Hotel before he was driven back to the airport. The next morning he flew home.

Several weeks later Kawamura and his chief engineer visited West Coast Cycle and stayed about three weeks. Day after day the trio toured bike shops, looking at bicycles, taking pictures, making drawings, talking to dealers. The engineer, Mr. Ikutaki, instantly understood why Japanese fenders, spokes and brakes quickly rusted in the salt air of coastal California, when the aluminum Swiss Weinmann brakes, for instance, didn't.

That wasn't enough. Howie bought fifteen bikes, including a Masi, a Colnago, several Schwinns, a Raleigh, enough to make a good assortment of high-end bikes representative of what was sold in American bike shops, and air-freighted them to Kawamura. A short time later, Howie followed the

McGann

shipment to Japan. When he arrived the bikes were already assembled, and Kawamura and his staff were studying them. Howie spent six weeks with Kawamura, going over the bikes, making sure they understood everything about what he needed.

A couple of weeks later, Kawamura was back in Los Angeles with still more questions and suggestions. After all of this travel and talk of components and design, no bikes had yet been made. Everyone was still learning, including Kawamura's getting to know more about Howie and West Coast Cycle and Howie's gaining a greater understanding of Kawamura's capabilities.

Howie couldn't explain what he wanted. He could only show Kawamura something that was well-made and ask that it be done on his bikes. It seemed to take forever and it wasn't until 1965 that, with a trembling hand, Howie signed a purchase order for 570 bicycles to be sold under his new American Eagle brand.

Kawamura couldn't have made money on that first shipment because there were so many models and colors in the hugely assorted shipment of 26-inch, 27-inch, 3-speeds, 10-speeds, boy's high-risers, girl's high-risers, and even a 16-inch-wheel convertible.

His consumer ten-speed, the American Eagle Olympic, used Shimano Eagle (a well-executed steel copy of the Simplex Export 61) derailleurs with big stem-mounted shift levers and a cottered Sugino steel crankset.

The Nishiki Olympic bike. Photo couresty of Broke Spoke Community Bike Shop, KY.

Why Your Bike Is Made in Asia

Because of the heavier tubing available to Japanese bike makers, at thirty-two pounds it weighed more than the European bikes (the Peugeot UO8 weighed 28 pounds), but was still ten pounds lighter than the Schwinn Varsity. Retail price was about $75.00.

The bikes were a smashing success. In just two weeks the shipment was sold out. The marketplace had confirmed Howie's vision of what a modern bike should be and what makers around the world had refused to produce: bikes that were reliable, comfortable, light and fairly priced. Surely the Japanese would have arrived at this point on their own, but with Kawamura's willingness to do whatever was needed to satisfy Howie's vision of the perfect bike for the American market and Howie's determined pedagogy, the learning curve was probably shortened by at least five years.

Howie and Kawamura weren't the only businessmen men advancing Japan's cause in the bicycle business. Two Japanese firms in particular had both outsized ambitions and the skills to match.

In 1921 Shozaburo Shimano began producing one-speed freewheels. Japan had a vigorous bicycle industry and despite a temporary shutdown in 1929 caused by the Great Depression, by 1939 Shimano was making more than a million freewheels a month.

The war destroyed Japan's cities and its productive capacity, American General Curtis LeMay's firebombing rendering all but five Japanese cities into burnt husks. On just one raid on March 10, 1945, LeMay had 325 B-29s firebomb Tokyo in a conflagration that killed 100,000 civilians. This savagery was replicated over and over until August of 1945 when Japan surrendered. Yet, by 1946, Shimano was up and running, producing freewheels as well as complete bicycles.

Seeking a way out of the economic chaos at the war's end, in 1949 Japan created the Ministry of International Trade and Industry (MITI), a powerful arbiter given the task of designing Japan's industrial policy. Driven to make Japan a modern industrial powerhouse, MITI displayed superb long-term planning as it decided which segments of Japan's economy would initially get what part of the scarce resources the flattened Japanese economy could deliver. First on MITI's list were steel, shipbuilding, chemicals and heavy equipment. This was nearly the same punch list as Soviet Union's under Lenin and Stalin, but the Japanese were far more successful.

In those first few years there was a general willingness among Japanese consumers to accept short and medium-term privation in order to advance their country's national interest. Japan's profits were plowed back into her economy while Japanese industrialists were willing to take on harrowing levels of debt to build and improve their factories.

Historian David Halberstam labeled the system the post-war Japanese evolved "a state-guided communal capitalism", depending on the Japanese tradition of the individual's subordination to the larger group. While the sacrificing worker would get little for his efforts, the harmony-breaking wealth-grabbing urges of the industrialists were also tempered. In the interest of the greater good, the wealth-concentrating tendencies of western capitalism were avoided. This was not a world congenial to Russian novelist Ayn Rand, but the results were startling. By the late 1950s the Japanese steel industry was the most advanced in the world.

Even more important than the investments in heavy industry was the government's drive to create engineers. Japan, like Italy, is largely bereft of natural resources. Japan would only be able to create wealth by investing in her people. The goal was to make sure that every person with a mechanical or mathematical gift had a chance at being a college-educated engineer. While America's best minds gravitated towards finance and management, Japan worked to make sure it had a higher proportion of engineers than any other industrialized nation, at the behest of Saburo Okita of the Economic Planning Agency. Even Japanese destined to be blue-collar workers received a rigorous education, strong in math and science, making them valuable and flexible parts of the ambitious nation's economy. With a multitude of engineers and well-educated workers, Japan planned to out-design, out-produce and out-think the rest of the world.

Shimano subscribed to this philosophy. After the war the company made sure 10 percent of its employees were engineers. Shimano discontinued complete bicycle production, and during the late 1950s and early 1960s had moved beyond freewheel production. Shimano began making several derailleurs, all of which were copies of European designs. By 1957 it had developed a 3-speed hub that avoided conflict with Sturmey-Archer's patents. It wasn't as robust as the fabled Sturmey-Archer AW, but it worked well enough and could be produced in Japan at low cost, all of which added up to Columbia using it on that Western Auto bike order.

In 1958, Shozo Shimano, eldest of Shozaburo's sons, took over after Shozaburo's death, and the company seemed even more driven to succeed. By 1965, Shimano had a sales office in New York and was furiously developing derailleurs for less expensive bikes. The new derailleurs were extremely successful. The other two Shimano brothers didn't just stay home and clip coupons. Keizo bossed the engineering and development side of

Why Your Bike Is Made in Asia

the company and Yoshizo (Yoshi) was sent to the U.S. to run Shimano's attempt to crack the American market.

After Yoshi's success in getting 3-speed hubs accepted by Western Auto, the Europeans gave him a key on a gold platter that opened the door to where he wanted to go more than anywhere else: Schwinn. In the 1960s Schwinn was the prestige American marque and getting spec'd on Schwinn bikes conferred instant validation and prestige.

Schwinn's Varsity and Continental 10-speed bikes came with French-made Maillard freewheels. With the bikes being targeted at twelve-to-fourteen year olds, it was no surprise that the French-made Maillard freewheels (the cluster of five sprockets on the rear wheel) would get fouled with dirt and sand. Schwinn asked Maillard if a plastic seal could be installed in the freewheel to keep out dirt, offering to pay more for the improvement.

Maillard refused, but thought themselves generous in making sure Schwinn knew that Maillard would be happy to replace any freewheel that went bad. A willingness to replace returned product is a crucial part of any decent customer-service program, but it can never be a substitute for making an item correctly in the first place.

Replacing a fouled freewheel involved an extraordinary amount of lost time and money. The bike owner's parent had to drive the bike to the shop and most likely leave it to be repaired. And possibly, because the child was without a bike, he would have to be driven to school. The dealer would remove and replace the freewheel and make sure the gears were adjusted. The parent would then have to drive back to the shop to pick up the repaired bike. Then, the dealer had to submit the freewheel to the Schwinn sales rep, who would write up a credit and perhaps take the greasy, dirty freewheel with him. Eventually the dealer got credit and, after submitting a request to Maillard, Schwinn would receive a replacement. All this because Maillard wouldn't add a two-cent plastic ring to the freewheel. This is why good companies that care about their brands and their customers are obsessed with quality-control and product reliability. It is always cheaper to do it right the first time.

Maillard's intransigence was incredibly expensive to both Maillard and the French component industry. I am sure Maillard knew that they made Europe's strongest freewheel and probably felt they had Schwinn over a barrel.

This drama wasn't occurring in a vacuum. As with Takei and RosaBelle Cohen, Yoshi Shimano had been making regular calls on Al Fritz, Schwinn's head of design and manufacturing. At one visit during the bike boom of the early 1970s, Fritz explained his frustrating freewheel problem to the Shimano brother. Soon Fritz had a sample of a sealed Shimano freewheel which was quickly spec'd on Schwinn 5- and 10-speeds.

Shimano took this little opening and drove a truck through it. Yoshi made it clear to Schwinn that he was there to solve their problems and developed a close working relationship with Schwinn. In 1974 Schwinn abandoned the Allvit for a much better shifting Shimano derailleur that was labeled "Schwinn Approved".

Earlier Schwinn had tried to use Campagnolo's Gran Turismo wide-range touring derailleur for its high-end touring bike. But the Gran Turismo is legendary for being a giant, beautifully chromed piece of steel that set new standards for poor shifting—Campagnolo's ventures beyond its core expertise in making road racing equipment have been generally unsuccessful.

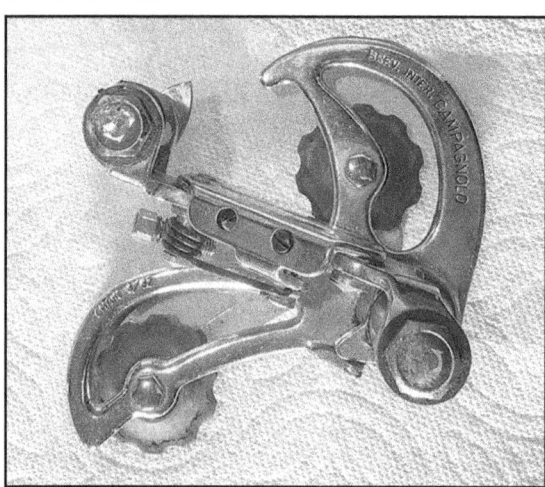

A used Campagnolo Gran Turismo rear derailleur

Shimano offered its excellent Crane GS as a Schwinn-branded derailleur. It is said that Campagnolo's Rally, a later derailleur that was an obvious Crane copy, was then offered to Schwinn. But Schwinn preferred the still better-working and lower-cost Crane. The most celebrated component manufacturer in the world had lost in its first shootout with Shimano. Life would not get easier for Shimano's competitors.

Shimano was doing so well that in 1970 a new factory, then the largest bicycle-oriented manufacturing plant in the world, was built in Shimonoseki, Japan. Employing more than 1,000 workers, including more than 100 engineers, Shimano was not only creating an extraordinarily wide range of products for low-end bikes, it was moving up-market as well. In 1973 Shimano announced its intentions to take on the best when it came

Why Your Bike Is Made in Asia

out with its Dura-Ace group. It was a complete component group with hubs, crankset, freewheels, brakes and derailleurs. Dura-Ace was world-class. The derailleurs, not quite as advanced as Japanese competitor SunTour's, still worked better than the highly vaunted Campagnolo changers.

Shimano was not done delivering shocks. Shimano became a title sponsor of one of Europe's finest professional teams. The Flandria-Shimano-Carpenter squad of 1976 included future 1981 World Champion Freddy Maertens (who holds the record for most professional bike road race wins in a single year), 1977 Giro d'Italia (Tour of Italy) winner Michel Pollentier, and 1969 Paris–Roubaix winner Walter Godefroot.

Much of Europe was aghast. Maertens and the other riders on the team were accused of being disloyal to European component makers. But professional bicycle racing is a business. Shimano had excellent components and could afford to become a title sponsor to the powerhouse squad. Walter Godefroot's stage-five victory in Spain's Ruta del Sol race in February of 1973 was the first European professional race won on a bike equipped with Japanese components. It would not be the last.

By 1974 Shimano was a publicly traded company with sales offices all over the world and had a huge range of well-designed products that benefited from a relentless, ubiquitous marketing campaign.

In the 1980s other Japanese companies including Hitachi, Toshiba, Miyata, Panasonic, Yoko, and Nissan would sponsor high-end European cycling teams.

Maeda was an Osaka freewheel company that had been around since 1912. Until 1964, Maeda, branding its product line SunTour, had been producing freewheels and knockoffs of French derailleurs. The company had begun selling derailleurs in 1956. That first effort, subcontracted out to Iwai Seisakusho, was named the "8.8.8. Wide" and could easily have been mistaken for a Huret Competition pull-chain derailleur. It was decently made, but nothing to cause competitors on the other side of the planet to lose sleep.

When Iwai Seisakusho went out of business in 1958, SunTour began making their own derailleurs (though many believe SunTour was still subcontracting its derailleur production). In 1960, still basically copying French designs, SunTour began making the Skitter. But, though it looked like a stamped steel version of Huret's Svelto, this derailleur was a powerful warning shot that the Japanese were not to be ignored. The first version (the rumor mill talks of Huret's making these derailleurs for SunTour, but I think that unlikely) didn't depart hugely from Huret's design, except that the adjusting screws were very easy to get to.

McGann

But, in 1964 SunTour came out with the Grand Prix (sometimes spelled "Gran Prix", even by SunTour itself). The Grand Prix was a giant improvement in the state of the art. Monumental, in fact.

SunTour had hired a genius, Nobuo Ozaki, to head its product development. Ozaki's brilliant insight was the slant parallelogram derailleur, first introduced with the Grand Prix. The top wheel ("jockey wheel") of the rear derailleur guides the chain during gear shifts as it moves across the freewheel cogs. One of the challenges derailleur designers face is keeping the jockey wheel at the optimum distance from the cog to get the crispest possible shift. With the traditional vertically-mounted parallelogram, the jockey wheel is too far from the small cog and on wider-range freewheels, too close to the big cogs. Even the best derailleur of 1964 shifted poorly.

With Ozaki's mounting the parallelogram at an angle on the New Skitter, the jockey wheel tracked the freewheel. Brilliant!

Few knew it at the time, but the SunTour Grand Prix was the best derailleur in the world. Though homely and only able to handle a 24-tooth freewheel, it could do it better than any other derailleur in the world.

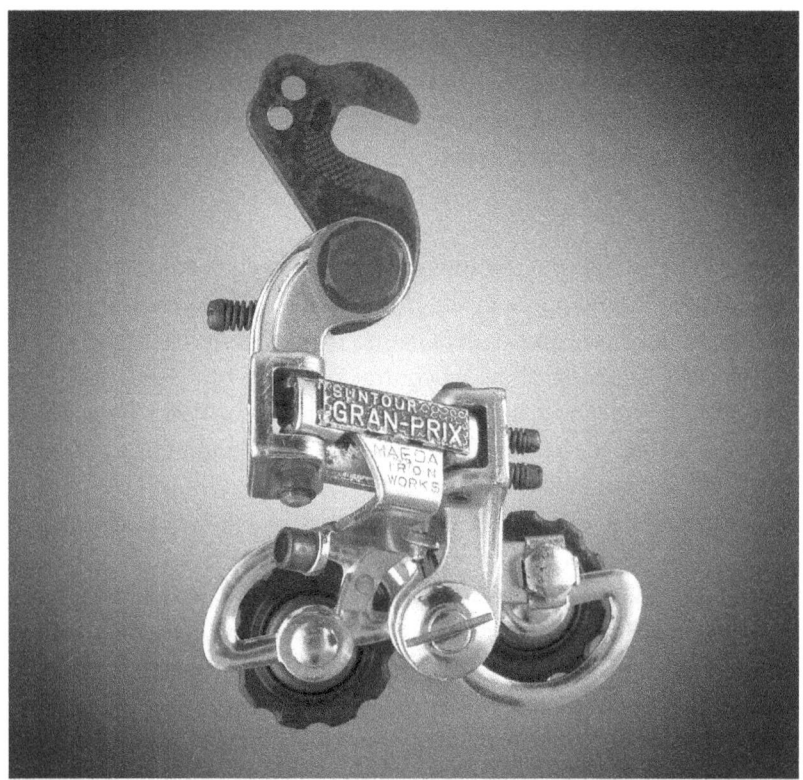

The SunTour Gran Prix rear derailleur. Photo courtesy of disraeligears.co.uk

Why Your Bike Is Made in Asia

The SunTour patent has long-since expired and all quality derailleurs are now slant parallelograms. The world soon found out how good SunTour derailleurs were. In 1970 SunTour sold 800,000 slant parallelograms and quickly became Japan's number one derailleur maker.

Both SunTour and Shimano continued to innovate and design products that suited their customers. The bikes Howie and others were bringing in from Japan had very low gears, usually a 32-tooth cog in the back to allow casual cyclists to get up nearly any hill. Japanese derailleurs handled these ultra-wide gears with ease. European bikes generally came with a 14-28 toothed freewheel, meaning the European bikes didn't have as low a gear. Worse, European derailleurs were at the limit of their capacity when mated with these freewheels and shifted poorly compared to their Asian counterparts.

Japanese component makers scored their biggest victory in the back rooms of bike shops. 1970s bicycle mechanics fell in love with Japanese parts, especially those made by SunTour. If a Simplex or Huret derailleur needed replacing, unless some configuration of the bike required otherwise, mechanics generally tried to replace them with SunTour. Japan's superior designs were first noticed and promoted by those who had to make the bikes of the bike boom work.

West Coast Cycle became a powerhouse distributor. Howie's American Eagle bike line was quickly renamed Nishiki. It became a huge seller all over the country.

Others jumped in. Mitchell Weiner had been managing Peugeot importer United Bicycle Sales for owner (and Weiner's father-in-law) Rudy Seidler before becoming an agent for Japanese manufacturers. Raleigh U.S.A. had Weiner produce a Japanese version of Raleigh's competitor to the Peugeot UO8, the Grand Prix (some of which had been produced by the Dutch Gazelle factory). When Raleigh of Nottingham, England, got wind of the deal, they quashed it, horrified at the thought of Japanese bikes carrying the storied Raleigh name, though some said Raleigh England was afraid the superior Japanese bikes would outsell British production.

Weiner was stuck with 2,000 bikes. While Raleigh was having its change of heart, Weiner had been reading Joseph Wambaugh's 1971 bestseller, *The New Centurions*. So the bikes, with their Raleigh Grand Prix style paint jobs got "Centurion" decals, and a famous bicycle brand was born. The bikes were well-made (vastly superior to the English-made Grand Prix, though the Dutch-made bikes were quite fine) and sold like hotcakes. Weiner was in business, selling Centurion bikes through his Western State Imports firm in California's San Fernando Valley.

The Japanese import trickle turned into a flood: Fuji, C.Itoh, Bridgestone, Sekai and Takara all contributed to the more than one million bikes a year that came into the U.S. during the bike boom.

5
Selling Brand X

The Brownian motion of my life that landed me in my bike shop that 1974 summer wasn't terribly different from that of the rest of my demographic cohort (now charmingly called "aging baby boomers"). More than a few of us took to opening bike shops in the early 1970s.

I was a ne'er-do-well. After graduating high school I worked as a busboy and dishwasher at London Heathrow airport, sold Fuller Brushes door-to-door, picked lemons, tutored high-school students, went to the local junior college for a couple of semesters, was a chauffeur, janitor and worked the graveyard shift at a gas station. I was going nowhere fast.

As I plied my aimless life, I returned to my bicycle. My father had given me a small (it must have had 20 x 1⅜" tires) lightweight English bike with a coaster brake when I was five (1956). He spotted it at the Pep Boys auto parts store on lower State Street in Santa Barbara and immediately bought it because it wasn't the usual fat-tired bike given to children of the era.

Since then bicycles have had a powerful grip on me. At one point I was the only guy who rode his bike to high school in the 1960s. Looking back, I can't really explain why I felt compelled to go to all the trouble caused by riding the bike, and why I was willing to stick out like a sore thumb from my peers, but ride my bike to school I did.

While I worked at my final real job, working graveyard at a Standard Station (owned and run by Standard Oil, not a Chevron franchised dealer), I started spending time in bike shops. The owners were all very generous with their time. I had no plans to spend any money. I just wanted to be in places that had bikes. I still remember a lost quarter hour staring at an all-Campagnolo bike at a local store in downtown Ventura, California. Campagnolo made a graceful cable guide that clamped to the downtube near the bottom bracket shell so that the cable went from the gear lever around the guide up to the front derailleur without the use of any cable housing. Compared to the primitive Huret Allvit on my bike, it was pure art.

McGann

The Campagnolo parts were graceful looking with all unessential material removed. The cable guide was a piece of perfect industrial design and I was enchanted. I know I returned several times to the shop just to admire the cabling of that front derailleur. If I hadn't seen bike-crazed people come into my own shop later on, simply to stare endlessly at bikes, I would still think myself crazy. Actually, I was and they were. But it was a fine madness.

I read everything I could find on bikes, but in the early 1970s there was little good information available to an American. There was a lot of questionable advice sold, such as the book I still have that advised men to use women's underwear to avoid chafing while riding, acquiring a pair of cycling shorts not being in the author's list of solutions. This author also concluded that the execrable Campagnolo Gran Turismo rear derailleur was the best wide range gear changer made. During the bike boom much was said and written, a lot of it dead wrong.

In 1974, still working at gas stations and living in a rented room at the back of a nice old lady's house, I decided to give junior college another shot with the goal of a business degree and a trip to law school. But the prospect of years of schooling and performing real work seemed daunting. More importantly my father wanted me close by as he struggled with poor health. Heck, I decided, why not do what I really wanted to do, and play with bikes?

When I told my parents of my plans for again stopping my college studies, this time to open a bike shop, I got nothing but encouragement. I had no idea how to go about starting a shop, but ignorance had never stopped me from feeling fully confident that I knew what I was doing (McGann's First Law: In a given individual, ignorance and certainty are directly proportional).

I had saved about $3,000 (about $19,000 in 2024 dollars) working at the gas station. This is where working for a company-owned Standard Station rather than a Chevron dealer mattered. Base pay for an employee at a company-owned station in 1972 was $5.25 an hour (that $5.25/hour translates to $33.00/hour in 2024 dollars) with double pay for federal holidays and extra pay for working the graveyard shift.

I will always be grateful to Mr. LeCroix. His large, friendly family welcomed me into their house when I was selling Fuller brushes in Ventura. I sometimes (read: usually) found the door-to-door work daunting and I discovered that when I stopped by the LeCroix house I was always given a welcome and a chance to chat for a short while before hitching up my pants and going back to knocking on doors. One day Mr. LeCroix, a wholesale sales representative for Standard Oil, said that he might be able find me

Why Your Bike Is Made in Asia

a better place to work and called the manager of the biggest company-operated Standard Station around and asked if there were any openings.

A kind man named Jim Lupold was the manager of Standard Station Number 576, just off the freeway in Ventura, and he said I should stop on by for a chat. After a short interview he said that a couple of his employees were headed off to college in a little more than a month and that I should check with him then. I found myself agreeing with Mr. LeCroix that this would be a better place to park my directionless self and stopped by at least once a week to see if there were an opening.

Mr. Lupold finally had a place for me. But before I could work there I was sent to Standard Station school. Standard Oil had a classroom in the San Fernando Valley where every employee spent a week learning the exact way to approach a car (the proper angle was important), solicit a full tank of gas, wash windows, check oil, and all the other things that used to be done by gas station attendants. Later I was sent to oil change/lube job school at the same place.

Not only did I get a job that paid well, I learned important lessons in customer service that would serve me well in the rest of my business life.

That was enough to give me a leg up on the costs of attending a state college in 1974, but not nearly enough to become a buyer and seller of bikes. And what kind of bikes to sell?

In early 1974 bike wholesalers were nearly all sold out. Letter after letter and phone call after phone call to distributors and manufacturers yielded absolutely nothing. I spotted an advertisement for Maserati bicycles imported by a Florida company called the Elsco Corporation. My memory is that the firm was owned by a former Maserati race car driver. Expecting the worst, I wrote to them.

Elsco's response gave me a thrill and a shock. They would sell me Maserati bicycles, but I would have to buy twenty-five units in a product mix of their choosing, sending me what, to my initial bafflement, was a "proforma" invoice. It including a healthy sprinkling of Maserati's upper end bikes. The bill came to about $3,500 and I had to prepay the order.

I didn't have $3,500. Where would Bill the Loser get his hands on that much money?

Someone told me I needed a business plan if I wanted to borrow money from a bank to buy inventory. I sat down with a pencil and yellow lined legal paper and drafted a projection of sales and expenses. I had no idea what I was doing and had no experience to base my plan on, but if a bank needed a business plan, I would do my best give them one. Looking back a year after I opened the shop, the plan had turned out to be rather accurate.

McGann

I put on my only pair of corduroys (bell bottoms, of course) without holes in the knees and my best shirt, an orange and blue rugby shirt, and started getting turned down.

I lived in Ventura, a beautiful city that stretches along the southern California coast, between Los Angeles and Santa Barbara. Starting at the east end, I worked my way across town, stopping at each bank to apply for a loan. I came close with one. The loan officer went so far as to keep my papers to see if the loan committee would bite. Nope.

I was told that because I didn't have a wife, children, house (Zorba the Greek's "full catastrophe"), my life didn't have enough stability, making me a poor credit risk. I uselessly countered that by living in the back of an old lady's house, riding a bike everywhere and not having a family to care for, I would have no distractions and almost no living expenses. I could focus all of my energy on the shop and needed to draw very little money out of the business while it was new and fragile. No dice.

I kept moving across the city until I was at the west end of town. I was about out of banks, city and hope. The ominous prospect of law school loomed darkly before me. There was a new bank in an ornate old building on the corner of California and Main (where Erle Stanley Gardner had written his early Perry Mason novels in an upstairs office), American Commercial Bank. It was the last unvisited Ventura bank. I squared my shoulders and walked into the old-fashioned, high-ceilinged lobby and explained my fool's errand to a lady at a desk and was told to talk to the loan officer.

I will never forget the courtesy Ken May showed me. He looked at my handwritten pages and the Maserati paperwork. He talked to me at length, probing into the nooks and crannies of my life and asked me to come back in a few days while he thought about my plan. When I returned, I learned Mr. May was an experienced banking executive who had been recruited by the less-than-one-year-old bank and had been given substantial authority in granting loans.

"I'm allowed a few mistakes," he told me. I started to shake all over with a surge of adrenaline, thinking I knew where he was headed. "We're going to loan you the money to buy the Maserati bicycles." To this day I remain grateful to this wonderful man who was willing to take a chance on me. He was a still a careful banker and issued a check payable to Elsco, not to me. I told him that even if the bike shop failed, I would pay back the loan in full, with all of the interest. "I know that," he said.

I mailed the bank's check off to Elsco and made other preparations to open my shop. I took my savings, negotiated a lease and paid first and last month's rent and bought an assortment of repair parts from Rudy Seidler's

Why Your Bike Is Made in Asia

United Bicycle Sales. My memory was that the parts bill came to $300.00. They all fit in the trunk and back seat of my 1964 Chevrolet Bel Air.

While I was painting the shop interior, boys interested in the new bike shop gathered at the front door. They asked me if I planned to sell BMX.

"What's BMX?" I asked. Really, I had no business being in this business.

The boys showed me their number plates, special handlebars and grips and explained that they took Schwinn Sting-Ray 20-inch bikes and modified them for jumping in the dirt.

That brought to mind a notice I had recently seen posted in the local Schwinn shop. It warned of a dangerous new fad, jumping 20-inch bikes in the dirt. Schwinn cautioned against any of their customers participating in this dangerous pastime and warned that failed parts showing evidence of having been abused in the dirt would not be eligible for warranty consideration.

This was quite a change from Schwinn's quick response to the early '60s fad of mounting polo seats, sissy bars and high-rise handlebars on 20-inch bikes. The company had responded almost instantly with the Sting-Ray, one of Schwinn's best-ever selling bikes. Since that rousing popular success, as shown by its response to the BMX fad, Schwinn's corporate culture had changed, stiffened. It turned out that Schwinn president Frank V. Schwinn was scared poo-less of the potential injuries and lawsuits caused by kids bouncing around on the dirt on Schwinn bikes.

BMX seemed like good clean (or muddy, depending on the season) fun to me. I told the boys I would find the equipment they wanted and carry it in my shop.

"Cool!"

After a few inquiries I was told to call Linda, of Linda's BMX. Shortly after calling, a young lady drove up in a well-stocked van and explained what I needed. I bought the equipment she recommended and was now a BMX shop.

I disassembled my own bike, a Windsor Professional made in Mexico, cleaned the Campagnolo parts, and carefully displayed them in a cheap bookcase I had purchased at the local Thrifty Drug store. I now had the Windsor frameset made from Columbus tubing and the better part of a Campagnolo groupset for sale to go along with my inventory of bikes.

My parents were concerned that I still didn't have enough product. It was now May and though I was ignorant of it (like nearly everything else), the bike boom had peaked and sales were slowing. Dad found French bike maker Gitane had an operation in Hawthorne, near Los Angeles, and asked if they would sell to me. They would, the salesmen offering him ten of their low-end Gypsy model equipped with steel cottered cranks, Mafac brakes and Simplex Prestige (yes, the plastic ones) derailleurs. Standard French bike boom fare.

A couple of days later a truck driver arrived at my parents' house with ten Gypsy bikes, demanding "ten-forty-two". My parents were in a panic, because they didn't have $1,042.00, the amount they assumed was needed to pay for the bikes. The truck driver, wanting to make the delivery and get on with his job, grew increasingly testy. "You mean you can't come up with a measly ten-forty-two?"

Eventually he figured out the problem and explained that he needed $10.42 to pay the freight bill and a personal check would do nicely. Gitane Pacific had shipped the bikes on open account, an amazing amount of trust, given that no credit application had been filled out, no papers had been signed. I assume their inventory was piling up and were glad to have a customer take ten Gypsys off their hands.

As I made my rounds to tell some of the shops in the area about my plans, I went by the Schwinn shop in Oxnard, the city next to Camarillo, to tell good-guy owner Dwayne Davenport my plans. In the shop I ran into the Schwinn sales representative who asked me what was going on.

"What brands are you going to sell?"

"Gitane and Maserati," I answered.

"Har! Another Brand X store!" Brand X was Schwinn-speak for any non-Schwinn bike brand. My, that felt good.

So, the situation in mid-1974, even with the bike boom coming to an end: American and European companies still dominated. Cheap department-store bikes were made in American factories that bought their mild-steel tubing by the mile and assembled them with components (excepting the derailleurs) that were made in the U.S.

European companies were prestigious and busy. France made 2.4 million bikes in 1974. They were unworried about, in fact were contemptuous of, their Asian competition which was steadily infiltrating the American market with a vastly superior product.

My memory of Bill's Bike Shop on that opening day in June of 1974 is still crystal clear. It was in a shopping center that had done poorly for years. Although it was anchored by a very popular grocery store, the landlord had never been able to lease out most of the small shops in an attached arcade. I signed a five-year lease for a 750-square-foot store front that had been a barber shop where a few years before I had had my hair cut. I filled

Why Your Bike Is Made in Asia

it with homemade fixtures and whatever I could scrounge up. The counter was a made of particleboard boxes bolted together and topped with a Formica counter my father had found gathering dust in a cabinet shop that a customer had never picked up. My showcases were those small glass-fronted bookshelves picked up at Thrifty Drug for almost no money. The bicycle workstand was a home-made device made from pony-pipe clamps that a friend had. The wheel-truing stand was a Japanese Hozan with a broken base. The wrenches and sockets were cheap tools from Builder's Emporium.

The Gitane and Maserati bikes were spread as far apart as would look seemly. I tried to make it look as if I had enough inventory to give a customer confidence that I would be in business tomorrow. In truth, if any shop looked like Brand X, it was Bill's Bike Shop in June of 1974.

Bill's Bike Shop in 1974

McGann

My genius marketing plan was to sell my labor cheap (complete bicycle overhaul for $12.95) and almost always be open for business. My hours were nine to nine, seven days a week, closed for Christmas and Easter. No one had to worry about my being closed. A customer could come to my store and I surely would be open. And if I came early or stayed late, the door would be open. Nothing ever made me more frustrated than coming to a store and seeing the owner busily going about his business, ignoring me until the second-hand crossed the opening time and then coming to unlock the door. That would never happen at any business I owned. I owed my customers who had gone to the trouble of coming to my shop that much respect.

Almost all the parts came from United Bicycle Sales, the Peugeot Importer. The United salesman made it clear that I would not be allowed to have Peugeot bikes because Camarillo Bicycle Center was the town's dealer. The West Coast Cycle representative went further, telling me that he would not even sell me parts because Camarillo Bicycle Center was giving him so much business. The omnipresent orange Nishiki bikes were imported by West Coast and though it pained me, not selling to me made perfect sense.

My opening parts inventory included Huret derailleurs, Weinmann brakes, Ejac cables, Rigida rims, Union spokes, chains and pedals, Maillard and Atom freewheels. They were among the premier parts makers of the age, all were giants of the industry. Several are still around, but are no longer the bike industry heavyweights they were.

I was busted. Besides paying for my meager stock, I had to put up first and last month's rent, a deposit with the State Board of Equalization as security for the sales tax I would be collecting, buy tools, paint and a million other things that quickly depleted that $3,000 I had managed to save pumping gas. I had a few coins in a change box that morning, and that was it for cash. If I wanted to buy a hamburger for lunch, I would have to sell something. To save still more money, I parked my car and traveled by bike. My morning ride was a forty-mile trip that included stopping at the bank in Ventura with the deposit of the previous day's sales.

About those Maserati and Gitane bikes. While overpriced, the Maserati bikes (produced by two legendary Italian factories, Olmo and Fiorelli) came with decent paint and were close to being completely assembled. It didn't take me long to learn that this was doing me no favor because, at least back then, European bike factories never greased the brake and gear cables. The bikes had to be partially disassembled and rebuilt with new cables, making for more work and expense.

On the plus side, the Maserati frames and cranksets were straight. To work well a bicycle frame must put the rider, front and rear wheels and

Why Your Bike Is Made in Asia

the bike's two vertical tubes, the head tube and seat tube, in the same plane. Otherwise the bike will not steer correctly and the necessary special positional relationship between the rear sprocket cluster and the front crankset will be upset, making for poor gear shifting.

Those Gitanes, on the other hand, were a handful. All bike boom mechanics became adept at getting the steel chainrings to run straight. Tools were made for the specific job of straightening steel chainrings and mine got a lot of use as I assembled the Gitanes.

The frames were nearly always bent. The simplest test was to string the frame and then cold-set it in the stand. It was ugly to watch, but a sorry bike could be made to run decently with a few tugs and grunts. Gitane placed an ad in the September 1975 issue of *Bicycling* magazine with a picture of the Gitane warehouse manager stringing a frame, intending to show the company's care about quality. To me the ad screamed about the company's quality problems.

"Stringing" a frame. The aim is to push or pull on the rear triangle on either side until the string is the same distance from the seat tube on each side. Frames didn't always come that way from the factory!

77

McGann

To make the Gitanes and some other European bikes work, after I closed the shop in the evening I would align the frames and then reassemble them.

Shortly after opening the shop I discovered a wholesaler, EBM, in nearby Santa Barbara, about fifty miles up the coast. They imported a nice assortment of parts and had an Italian-made private-label bike line, Romana, which was well made. Owner Jim Myers opened at eight in the morning. I could be there waiting for him to open his warehouse to pick up an order called in the day before. He would help me load my car with the order first thing upon opening and I could pull up to my shop with parts and Romana bikes just before it was time to open the bike shop at nine. Jim Myers was kind, lovely person who was always ready to do what he could to help me. Before EBM closed its doors (another victim of the end of the bike boom) I was picking up an order almost every week. The fast inventory turns of his products made my few dollars go yet a bit further.

I toodled along, selling mostly Gitanes. The Maseratis' stiffer price made the Gitanes more attractive to people just looking for a bike to while away a few weekend hours. After a few months, the Raleigh sales rep came by and asked me if I wanted to be a Raleigh dealer. I considered Raleigh bikes the *summum bonum*. To think that I could sell Raleigh bikes was a knee-weakening thought. It turns out Chuck, over at the Camarillo Bicycle Center, was doing such a wonderful job selling Nishikis and Peugeots, Raleigh was neglected. Without thinking twice, I jumped at the chance. I would have to buy fifty bikes, but I could get extended payment terms. I was also told I'd have to carry the full line, and not "cherry pick" my bikes. I didn't know it at the time, but "carry the full line" and "not cherry pick" was sales department code for being forced to buy some of the company's dogs along with the good bikes. I didn't care. I was going to be a Raleigh dealer!

The bikes arrived. Instead of enjoying the unmitigated delight of having fifty fine English racing bikes to sell, assembling the Raleighs was a nightmare. The basic consumer 10-speed, the Record, was a piece of junk.

Until just a few years ago, quality bike frames were made of steel tubes joined with steel sockets called lugs. The builder heats the joint with a torch and uses molten brass that flows between the lug and the tubes to make a secure bond. Good builders make sure the brass flows throughout the joint without gaps between the lugs and tubes. In my shipment were Raleigh Records with gaps so large that on some bikes I could stick my thumbnail between the lug and the tube. Worse, the pedals had plain bearings. Honest, just a greased shaft, no ball bearings.

Why Your Bike Is Made in Asia

Some had ancient three-piece steel hubs, instead of modern one-piece forged aluminum hubs (like the Normandy hubs on the Peugeots and Gitanes, and Suzue on the Nishikis). Of course the frames and chainrings were bent. If I had possessed a little backbone and a better moral sense, I would have sent the bikes back and continued selling the still sorry, but higher quality Gitanes.

While researching this book I talked to another old dealer and lamented that I was surely going to Hell when I died. He asked me the cause of this grim theological insight. "I betrayed my customers' trust and sold Raleigh Records during the bike boom."

His not-so comforting response: "You'll have lots of company. We're all guilty and we're all going to burn."

People helped me. Friends came and bought bikes those first few days when it mattered most. When I accepted a Shimano 3-speed hub for repair and couldn't figure out how to fix it, Dwayne Davenport, owner of that Schwinn Shop in the next town, stopped by after work and schooled me in internal-geared hub repair.

I quickly learned the difference between an amateur like me, working on his own bike, and a professional bike mechanic like Dwayne who could quickly repair complex machinery like a 3-speed hub. It turns out I wasn't half as smart or knowledgeable as I thought I was. Working all alone in my shop forced me to learn a lot really fast, but it was years before I was an accomplished mechanic.

Besides all the other help Schwinn gave its dealers, the company produced the finest bicycle repair manual on the planet. A friend who had worked at that famous Helen's Cycles in Santa Monica gave me his copy. That lifesaver became a greasy, well-worn manual that I passed on to the gent who bought my shop in the 1980s.

With the closing of the Camarillo Bicycle Center, I picked up Peugeot. They came almost completely assembled, protected by a thick plastic bag that was shrink-wrapped around the bike. The cables were always kinked and lacked grease, so the bike had to be partially reassembled.

I now had a wide range of European bikes: Peugeot, Raleigh, Gitane. Often, because of the collapse in the bike market, the Raleighs and Gitanes could be purchased from the distributor at a big discount. In fact, some shops bought Campagnolo-equipped Raleigh high-end bikes just for the parts, and sold the frames (made from expensive Reynolds 531 tubing) for a pittance.

Other importers, large and small, were hammered by the sales collapse. A company in the San Francisco Bay area, the Murphy Company, imported some of the cycling's greatest and most famous brands. Mr. Murphy (a true gentleman who made doing business with his firm a pleasure) was forced to sell his wonderful stock for peanuts.

I still remember a man who would come by occasionally in the evening to talk bikes. He wore a trench coat and dark glasses and would sit down in the chair next to my desk (that had been left in the building by a previous occupant; I got my fixtures where I could. I gave the desk a coat of the same white house paint I had used to paint the store walls, gifted interior decorator that I was) and talked of his time racing in Europe. He would bring French racing magazines and clearly knew more about the sport than anyone I had ever met.

When he learned I could get a Legnano Roma Olimpiade racing bike from the Murphy Company for a song, he asked me to get one for him. The Roma Olimpliade (known as the Tipo Roma before Ercole Baldini won the 1956 Melbourne Olympic road race on one) is a bike of legendary fame. Painted in Legnano's traditional and distinctive yellow-green, the Campagnolo-equipped bike was built in Milan by Emilio Bozzi. Getting such a bike on the cheap was an opportunity not to be missed.

When the bike came, this gentleman examined the bicycle carefully and came back the next day with dated, though fine cycling clothes and gave it a thorough test ride, intelligently riding it with no hands to make sure the bike was properly aligned.

He bought the bike and after that I may have seen him only a couple of more times. I later learned that my customer, Martin Deras, was the American 1939 road racing champion. He never told me about his substantial accomplishments when bike racing was almost a relic of a forgotten time; modest, fine gentleman that he was.

As the bike boom wound down, importers found themselves saddled with inventories that took a long time to unload. SunTour "Spirt" [sic] front derailleurs were offered by wholesalers for under three dollars for years. It might have been 1977 that the country's surplus inventory of this useful and reliable derailleur was finally sold off. Spirts started costing me closer to the five dollars that gave the importer a reasonable profit. I threw a hissy fit that day.

Some time in my second year in the shop, my Peugeot sales representative was hired by Mitchell Weiner's Western States Imports. He offered me Centurion bikes, made in Japan. I hesitated because I had based my entire business on the superiority of the European cycling culture. Selling Centurions would be a sharp break. I tried a few of Centurion's basic model, the Le Mans. The aluminum cotterless cranks,

Why Your Bike Is Made in Asia

SunTour derailleurs and Dia Compe center-pull brakes were mounted on straight frames with good paint jobs. I was able to assemble them quickly and found they worked flawlessly. These were damn good bikes. These facts ran counter to my bike ideology, forcing me to become a convert. Very quickly my sales floor was covered with Centurions with a sprinkling of Peugeots for those customers who were more comfortable with the well-known brand.

The Centurion Le Mans

From the beginning I had offered two years of free adjustments with every bike I sold. Changing to Centurions significantly reduced the amount of labor I had to give away. They went out the door and didn't come back except for flat tires.

In the late 1970s, even after my success with Centurions, I believed that European enthusiast bikes (sometimes called semi-pro bikes) were still better than their Japanese counterparts, so I continued to enthusiastically sell PX10s, Peugeot's all-Reynolds double-butted tubing bike that could suit any rider stuck with a limited budget but wanting to compete.

In fact, Peugeot made a point that their professional team rode those same PX10 bikes I sold in Bill's Bike Shop. They were the same bikes, except for the Peugeots built by Italian master builder Faliero Masi for Eddy Merckx (who also used Campagnolo cranks instead of the flexible stock Stronglight model), Tom Simpson and other Peugeot team members who wanted something better than the dated equipment the tight-fisted

McGann

French company gave their riders. Merckx said the bikes the factory gave them "...rode like dogs".

To fix this glaring and obvious problem, Peugeot opened a special framebuilding shop to produce the PY10 for their professional riders, which could also be custom ordered for retail customers. On this fine bike Bernard Thévenet won the 1977 Tour de France. But at $250.00, the PX10 was an excellent value and rode well for the money, Merckx's disdain notwithstanding.

There was another problem with European bikes. Each country's cycling industry, starting in the nineteenth century, grew up isolated from each other. Stiff import duties that existed until the European Common Market was established kept Italians buying Italian bikes and Frenchmen buying French-made bikes. This resulted in different specifications for each country's parts. Italian bikes used one size and thread in its bottom brackets (the crankset bearings), the French another, while the British used several. And the Swiss? They used French threads but the drive side had left-handed threads (left-handed drive-side threads in a bottom bracket are actually superior, but that's not the point here). French bicycle tubing and handlebars were a different diameter. French freewheels were incompatible with British hubs, Italian freewheels were sort of interchangeable with British spec'd production.

The result? A bike shop had to carry French and British headsets, stems, bars, freewheels, countless bottom bracket parts. It was a crazy-quilt legacy dogging the entire industry. The Japanese cut the Gordian Knot by using British dimensions for all of the their bikes. Most Centurion repair parts worked on Nishikis, Panasonics as well as Schwinn lightweights and Raleighs. Italian parts were usually close enough that Japanese parts could be used to replace them.

The Gitane operation in Hawthorne, California could have been the start of something special. The frames were imported along with the other parts, which were partially assembled there in the Hawthorne warehouse. Here was a chance to produce a high-quality product. Frames could have been aligned, cranks checked, wheels built straight and true. It didn't happen. Mylar decals were stuck on crooked frames and the shoddy bikes were shipped to cycle shops, each becoming an eloquent salesman for Japanese bikes.

It was about 1977 when a gentleman named Tom French came by my shop with frame samples from a new American factory, Trek. They appeared to be well-made and nicely finished. And instead of the tight racing geometry

Why Your Bike Is Made in Asia

of the frames made in Europe, these had slightly longer wheelbases and more relaxed angles to make a more stable ride. Eyelets on the front and rear fork ends allowed riders to mount racks and equip their bikes for touring. I took a chance and bought three. The frames took a while for me to sell. They were silver-soldered rather than brazed with traditional brass. The argument for silver soldering is that the silver flows at a lower temperature, resulting in less harm to the frame tubing. All three had joint failures when the silver-soldered joints broke loose. Trek made good on all three, but that was enough for me. And a side note, tubing manufacturers assume frames will be brass-brazed and account for that when making their tubing.

Despite that hiccup, as a result of superb management and a good instinct for what Americans wanted to buy, the Wisconsin company went bravely on without me. Trek went from strength to strength and by the 1990s had far surpassed Schwinn in sales. Trek showed that the failure of American and European producers to compete with Asian factories was not the fault of location or workforce. As is nearly always true, the suits in the upstairs offices were to blame.

6
Kids really want to play on their bikes

What about those BMX (bicycle moto-cross) boys? Since the Schwinn Sting-Ray's release in 1963, kids had reveled in the bike's limitless fun potential. With small wheels, short wheelbase, stable geometry, and bullet-proof construction, rough and tumble play in the dirt was a natural. When the opening scenes of the 1971 motorcycle motocross movie *On Any Sunday* showed kids riding in the dirt on Sting-Rays with number-plates, imitating the motorcyclists, boys everywhere had their imaginations fired.

But as strong as those Schwinn parts were, they weren't up to the rigors of racing in the dirt. Riders discovered they went faster with longer crankarms, but the Sting-Ray's low bottom bracket made cornering difficult, especially with longer cranks.

In the early '70s, the first custom BMX frames were fabricated. Sometime shortly after I opened my shop, a teenager asked me if I could get him a Webco. I had no idea what a Webco was, but he was ready. He handed me an advertisement in one of the early BMX publications. It was for a 20-inch frame specially made for BMX. I made the call and in a few days I had what was probably the first production BMX frame, made from mild steel, by Webco. Webco had so far been a motorcycle parts supplier, but its owner had a son who rode BMX (a not uncommon thread in the BMX industry). The frame had a higher bottom bracket and a reinforcing gusset at the head tube.

Another BMX dad in the motorcycle business, Linn Kasten, started a brilliant run. Finding component after component unsuitable, he began making parts out of high-strength chrome-moly steel, instead of the lower-strength mild steel then used in nearly all bicycle manufacturing.

Kasten's son had the same complaints about the existing bikes every other kid had: the bottom bracket on the Sting-Ray was too low, the frame too heavy. For Christmas of 1973, Kasten built a bike using a frame he TIG-

85

welded out of chrome-moly steel. The higher-carbon steel allowed him to use lighter, thinner tubing, yet still end up with a stronger frame.

Word of Kasten's frame got out. He ended up at one of the early Meccas of BMX, Pedalers West Bike Shop in Southern California's San Fernando Valley. In the early 1970s shop owner Jim Emerson had been modifying Royce Union girls' frames by welding on a reinforcing top tube, making the best of what was available. Emerson was taken by Kasten's bike, but told him there was a bigger problem than inadequate frames. The kids were breaking the forged Ashtabula forks that came on Schwinns left and right, sometimes getting hurt in the process.

Emerson asked if Kasten could make a stronger fork. While driving back home, the solution came to him: the tubular steel fork. He would weld fork blades of chrome-moly steel tubes directly to the steering tube. Kasten was sure it would work because that was how airplane nose gears were made and the loads and impacts seemed to him very much the same.

Kasten came back with his prototypes. The reaction to Kasten's very different-looking forks was negative. No one will want these forks, he was told, they were too big and heavy. That was, until they picked one of his forks up. These ponderous-looking forks were really light! The kids couldn't wait to try to break them. They gave it everything they had, but Kasten's forks could take it all. Jumping and wheelie-ing that had reduced the traditional forged forks to scrap metal couldn't hurt the new forks, thanks to the magic of thin-wall, high-strength steel.

The RedLine BMX bike, showing the tubular fork

Why Your Bike Is Made in Asia

Soon Kasten's RedLine Engineering was making forks by the truckload. But he didn't get his design patented. He was told patenting it would cost thousands of dollars, which the young engineer didn't have, and success was doubtful. Soon imitators sprung up, eventually not only on BMX bikes, but also on mountain bikes and road bikes, where, with some changes, Kasten's original design was sold as a Unicrown fork. He also designed and made motocross-style handlebars and a double-clamp stem that would neither break nor allow the handlebars to slip.

He put his frame, bars and stem into production as well. The forks were a big hit and after his original distributor ran into trouble, Kasten ended up talking to Howie Cohen of West Coast. Cohen didn't think much of the clunky-looking forks and turned down an opportunity to distribute them. Later, after Howie had left the firm in 1976, West Coast became an important RedLine distributor.

Earlier, Japanese trading company Marui (in general, importers buy Japanese goods from a trading company, which handles all the commercial details as well as shipping) had taken several BMX company managers on a tour of Japanese factories, mostly with the hope of selling them Shimano components. Kasten was struck by what he saw. He wondered about the wisdom of competing against these firms should they decide to invade the BMX market.

In early 1978 Kasten decided to have his frames and forks fabricated in Japan and then have the framebuilder assemble the bike from the Japanese parts Kasten was already importing. At this point Kasten was looking to streamline what had grown into a complex logistical manufacturing endeavor. He was making components and frames as well assembling complete bikes. The trouble was, he was just building four parts and importing thirty-three.

Howie put him in touch with Kawamura. Kasten found the Japanese builder fully up to making the high-quality bikes he needed to be good enough for the RedLine name. Kawamura was eager to make RedLines.

There was one big problem. The Japanese, for all of their technical expertise and cutting-edge steel industry, did not TIG weld. A quick explanation. TIG, or tungsten inert gas welding, has been around since the 1940s. It uses a tungsten electrode to create an electric arc to heat the metal while the joint being welded is protected from the atmosphere with an inert gas, usually argon. The inert gas prevents the welded material from reacting or combining with gases in the air, making for a stronger joint. With a foot pedal controlling the voltage, a skilled welder can join very thin pieces of metal such as the tubes of a bike frame.

Kawamura had no TIG welding machinery, nor could modern TIG welding machines be acquired in Japan. Under strictest secrecy, Kasten ordered American-made TIG welders and had them shipped to Kawamura. They were locked in a room in the Kawamura factory with a sign that said entry was only by permission of "Linn-San". In that room Kasten trained six Japanese men in the fine art of TIG welding. It took him about six months, but he ended up with four skilled welders who could produce lightweight steel frames and forks. From 1978 to 1983 Kawamura made RedLine frames, forks and bikes. Soon, other Japanese firms were producing well-made BMX frames, forks and complete bikes. Still, Kasten continued to produce frames, stems, forks, handlebars and whatever his fertile imagination came up with in the U.S. Only the complete bikes were made in Japan. The components and framesets were still domestically produced.

Years before 10-speed bike manufacturers dared abandon lugs and build TIG-welded frames, Kasten showed that high-strength steels could be welded to make light, rugged, good-riding and reliable frames that could take anything.

In the mid-1970s a whole new industry had grown up, almost overnight, to fill the need for bikes that could survive jumping and crashing yet be light enough for competition. It was an American industry, for now.

While the Japanese were carving out a serious portion of the world's adult bike market for themselves, another player came on the scene. Just as the reputation for immediate post-war Japanese goods was poor, any bike product made on the island of Taiwan in the mid-1970s was generally held in contempt. Western States Imports had brought in a Taiwanese-made bike around 1977, and like those early Japanese bikes Howie described, they were worse than department-store bikes.

Early on, there was an outlier, a factory called KHS. But success still didn't come easily to them. KHS had been making motorcycles in Taiwan under license from Yamaha as well as assembling Yamaha musical instruments. During the bike boom KHS decided to make lightweight consumer road bikes, probably the first Taiwanese maker to enter that market. In its first attempt, KHS failed miserably. The poor materials and workmanship instantly gave the bikes a terrible reputation. Realizing the extent of the catastrophe, KHS stopped export production and sought technical assistance from the Japanese.

The Sukosha Bicycle Company provided KHS with an engineer who spent five years with KHS. The result was a re-designed bicycle line made with modern equipment, including electrostatic painters and automatic

Why Your Bike Is Made in Asia

brazing machinery. More than that, KHS sent workers to Japan to learn how to use this state-of-the-art tooling. KHS was also careful, selling these new bikes in Taiwan for two years before re-entering the U.S. market.

Around 1975, KHS opened a warehouse in Southern California stocked with three inexpensive models of road bikes. The re-introduction of the line was a complete success. To this day, the company is a serious power in both the American and world bike market. And of course, other Taiwan factories followed.

Giant Manufacturing Co., a bicycle company started in 1972 by King Liu, was concerned about the various Taiwan component makers, worried that if some standard of quality were not followed, the island's bike makers would not be able to crack the higher end market. The ambitious Taiwan factory owners understood the logic of King Liu's argument, and standards were set and followed.

And there was quite a way to go for many Taiwan firms. John Neugent, who was managing importer Service Cycle in the early 1980s, remembers the primitive conditions he found at the Merida factory in Taiwan, saying it was just short of having dirt floors. Merida tried to make their product look Japanese, but their production was nowhere near Japanese quality. But Merida, like Giant and KHS and many others, was dedicated to cracking the quality nut. They did learn to make good product and along the way, KHS lost its primacy to Merida and Giant.

Both the Japanese and Taiwan bike makers showed an unbending dedication to conquering the U.S. bike market, understanding that they would have to out-build their prestigious European and American competitors if they were to succeed.

Soon after I opened my shop I started receiving flyers from a new company, Specialized Bicycle Imports, owned by Michael Sinyard. He would turn out to be the industry's most gifted and capable merchant, perhaps the best bicycle businessman of all time.

In 1974, while I was opening my bike shop, Sinyard sold his Volkswagen bus to pay for a cycling trip in Europe. Later, in an interesting parallel, Steve Jobs would also sell his VW bus to buy parts for the first Apple computer.

While in Italy Sinyard made contact with Cinelli and upon returning to the US, he placed his first order for the famous bars and stems. Incredibly, Cinelli granted the nearly broke Sinyard credit terms. He quickly turned the order, being happy with a slender 15 percent mark-up. In those lean first years, the tall, slender Sinyard lived in a trailer, sharing expenses with two friends. He was the real thing, a man truly committed to bicycles. He had no car. He would ride his bike from San Jose to the San Francisco airport to pick up his first shipments, a 140-mile round-trip.

I had a pathological love of high-end bike parts, which at that time could be hard to come by in America. Sometimes one of the big importers would get in a few Cinelli stems or Regina freewheels. I have no idea why we coveted Regina freewheels, but a gold-colored Regina Oro freewheel was something we all wanted on our bikes, despite their not being very good. But supply was always spotty. Somehow, Sinyard could get even the most difficult and rare product out of Europe. He proved it when he filled an order of mine for twenty Pogliaghi framesets (another legendary marque whose reputation vastly exceeded its quality), and rarest of all, two Cinelli Supercorsa bikes.

Sinyard wasn't content being just a middleman hustling to get Italian racing parts. In 1976 he introduced the Specialized Touring Tire, a Japanese-made clincher tire with a raised center section. Sinyard's design and marketing were brilliant. It was the perfect product at the perfect time. Most riders then considered themselves "tourists" and the tires available at the time were generally unsatisfactory. Nearly all of my serious customers demanded the Specialized tire.

Bicycles were changing. Until the mid-1970s, any racing cyclist had to use tubular or "sew-up" tires. This was a design that went back to John Dunlop's first pneumatic tires. The inner tube was sewn into the tire casing and the finished tire was glued onto a slightly concave rim. Sew-ups were fast, but expensive, and messing with the glue was a lot of trouble. Having a zealot's passion, I was generally unsympathetic to my customers who wanted a high performance bike yet hated sew-ups.

In 1973 Mavic (the French company that made the first aluminum rims in the 1930s) came out with a narrow clincher rim with a hook bead that would hold the tires without their exploding off the rim when inflated to higher pressures. Called the Module E, it was followed soon by French rim maker Rigida's ultra-narrow 13-20. At the same time, Michelin had developed their Elan high pressure tire. While the Elan was fragile, wore quickly, and was prone to blow-outs, performance riders were at last freed from the tyranny of sew ups. Like all shops, I did a huge business re-lacing hubs with the new clincher rims.

Shortly after the fragile Elans showed up, the French company Wolber introduced the W20, a much finer, stronger and better-riding tire. Note that it was French companies who were still making the important changes.

But it was Mike Sinyard who took the high-performance clincher and made it sing. A bit off-key at first, but sing it did when Specialized

Why Your Bike Is Made in Asia

came out with the Turbo in 1978. His Turbo tire had a Kevlar fiber bead, making the Turbo both much lighter by doing away with the steel wire bead, and foldable, which made it easier to carry and store. The first tires were execrable. The beads were so tight mechanics would break tire irons trying to mount them. And woe betide the rider who got a flat tire with those early Turbos, wrestling the tire off and back on the rim was not for the faint-hearted. Still, it was the state-of-the-art tire and it was made in Japan and people bought them by the ton. Quickly the Turbo bead problem was rectified and people could confidently ride down the road knowing an inexpensive flat tire could be easily repaired by the side of the road.

There was an important lesson that I absorbed imperfectly. In fact, I would have to re-learn it over and over and over again. I think it was in 1975 at a west coast bike trade show. A frame I had never heard of, Gios Torino, was on display in the booth shared by an importer calling himself Monty of Italy. The other occupant of the booth was 1984 Olympic road race gold medalist Alexei Grewal's father's Sherpa Sports.

The Gios frames were stunning. They were the only frames I had ever seen that could match Masi, surely the most perfectly built frames of the 1960s and '70s. I placed an order on the spot. When they arrived, the local racers came by to have a look. Until then, with but few exceptions, they were all deep believers in the superiority of Schwinn Paramount bikes. That Schwinn guarantee was a powerful aphrodisiac that seemingly no amount of reason could overcome. But, the Gios frames won them over. The perfect workmanship, magnified by Gios' early use of investment-cast (also called lost-wax process) parts and a lovely distinctive blue paint made them irresistible. I sold several that first week.

I got behind the frames, stocking a full size run in my little shop and equipping the best riders on the bicycle team I sponsored with Gios bikes. Soon I had racers coming up from Los Angeles to buy Gios frames from me. My little shop was selling a Gios frame or bike a week. I was in heaven. This is what I wanted to do, sell and build hand-made racing bikes.

Then one day it was over. My expensive rack of framesets just stood there. No takers. I asked around and found that a shop eight miles away, in the next town, was selling Gios frames at cost to build his business. I called the distributor to chew on him, and he feigned surprise. He clearly thought he could have both shops selling his frame. I explained (as I would to manufacturers for years to come), that he hadn't added to his retail locations, he had merely changed area retailers.

McGann

I dumped my stock. Soon thereafter the fellow in the next town, now that I no longer promoted the frames and with no one to undercut, dropped them as well.

Okay, for a short period of time I learned to not put the full force of any marketing effort behind something I didn't control. It may be my shop, but it's always the other guy's product.

I get things in my head. For years, the only source of European cycling news and pictures I could get my hands on was the now-defunct British publication, *International Cycle Sport*. ICS regularly had an ad for MKM frames, a company jointly owned by the king of British racing parts distributors Ron Kitching, in partnership with retired racers Wes Mason and Arthur Metcalf.

The frame pictures were stunning. I had to have these bikes for my shop. I talked to the importer of Follis, a respected, and now defunct French bike maker, to see if he would bring them in, promising him an order. George Linder's Linder-Euro Imports came through and I dutifully bought some for my shop in 1975. They had lovely baked enamel paint jobs, the sort that made other British makers like Bob Jackson famous.

Linder-Euro didn't long survive the end of the bike boom, but I still had MKM on the brain. I wrote to them, asking if they would sell directly to me. Of course MKM, now owned by a gentleman name Ian Crabtree, would sell to me. I placed an order for several, which eventually arrived by mail. This must have been sometime in 1976. I was now an importer. But the lesson of the Gios frames still stung. I didn't import these frames as MKMs. I brought them in without decals and labeled them Vulcan, after the Roman metalworker to the gods. Again, I took off down a road without

The unhappily-named Vulcan frameset

Why Your Bike Is Made in Asia

looking at the map. When they heard the name "Vulcan", people didn't think of the god of fire and blacksmithing. Instead, they laughed at the bikes because Mr. Spock of Star Trek came from the planet Vulcan.

When that name didn't work, I should have then picked a better one, but I was stubborn. For years I tried to sell frames with a name people weren't crazy about.

It might have been 1978 or 1979 when a burly, bearded, but kindly man with a very different-looking bike visited the bike shop. Gary Klein had what I believe to be the first TIG-welded aluminum bike made with oversized tubing. The bike and his company that produced them were the outgrowth of a design project he had pursued as a student at MIT. Aluminum bikes had been around since at least the 1930s, but they had problems. Although light, they would break, and since they were usually built with the same tubing diameter as used on steel bikes, they were very flexible, too soft for most riders' tastes. Klein's huge tubes solved that problem. His thoughtful choice of alloys and proper heat-treating after welding made them reliable enough to sell.

I took Klein's bike for a spin. It about jumped out from under me, it was so stiff and light. A closer examination of the bike showed Klein had stacked the deck a bit. The cranks were very long and the wheels were super light with special Italian racing silk tires. Those things aside, Klein's bike was different. It was expensive, but he was on to something. I thought the bike's oversize tubing made the ride far too harsh, but many others disagreed. His bikes were a hit and deservedly so.

To fast-forward a bit, in 1983 Cannondale, which had so far made backpacks and bike trailers, began making a Klein-type aluminum bike. But instead of retailing for $2,000, a Cannondale frameset (frame and fork) sold for $350.00. Klein, having patented his frame design, found little amusing about the Cannondales and filed suit in 1985. It was a hard-fought lawsuit, but in 1989 the Federal Court of Appeals upheld Cannondale's right to produce oversized aluminum-tubed frames. Klein eventually had to sell his increasingly financially troubled company to Trek in 1995. In 2001 the Klein factory in Washington State was closed and production moved to Trek's home base in Waterloo, Wisconsin. Sometime around 2006, the market for premium aluminum bikes having dried up, Klein production was discontinued.

Meanwhile, Cannondale began selling scads of their bikes, producing nearly all of them in their Bedford, Pennsylvania factory.

7
Moving from retailer to wholesaler

By 1981 I was a married man with a serious ongoing commercial concern. For some reason, a mutual friend who taught biology at nearby Moorpark College thought his fellow biology instructor Carol Schwalm might find me interesting. Why he thought this beautiful college graduate with a masters degree might want to meet me, a man with an indifferent high-school education, still remains a mystery to me. But she did consent to go out with me and in 1978 we were married in a simple ceremony in my parents' home. By then, Carol had become head of the biology department and had cycle-toured the entire California coast.

We turned out to be good business partners. She immediately started fixing up the bike shop. Parts strewn in the showcases were neatly arranged and given, for the first time, price tags. The frightening pile of unanswered correspondence on my desk was dealt with. Bills were paid on time and within a few weeks, this lovely, petite blond had turned my avocation bordering on a hobby into a real business.

I remained consumed with a desire to become an importer and distributor of high-end racing products. In 1981 I asked Carol if she wanted to make the leap with me. "Do you want to do this?"

"Sure," she replied, having as little idea as I had of what that one word would get us into. Her business courage and willingness to take chances were extraordinary. We needed capital, so she withdrew her retirement savings from her years of teaching at Moorpark College and made that hard-earned sum available to buy wholesale stock.

In January of 1981 we took off for Italy to see what we could find. English frames were not what the country wanted. Given the foreign currency exchange rates, I was convinced a good-selling entry-level Italian sport bike could be built. We had been in correspondence with a fine old Italian company, Torpado of Padua. We had a difficult time when we visited their factory because they spoke no English and at the time, we were just as useless in Italian. We managed to get our needs understood and were given some attractive tentative pricing.

But it all broke down because they said they disbelieved in the existence of 20-foot ocean shipping containers (sometimes called "cans" in the trade). A 20-footer holds 150 bikes, both the limit of our piggy bank and as many bikes as I was willing to risk importing at one crack. The 300 bikes that would fill a normal 40-foot can were beyond us. We were basically asking them to take two of their stock models and paint them up as Torelli bikes, the name we had chosen for our bicycle line. It would have entailed little disruption to their production.

We talked and talked but got nowhere. Finally, we thanked them for their time and trouble and asked them to call a taxi for us. I didn't know it at the time, but Torpado had been the maker of Ben Lawee's Italvegas, a highly respected private-label bike line, from 1970 until sometime in the late '70s. Always on top of market trends, Lawee then began his new line, Univega, switching to Japanese-made bikes. Given the trouble I had with the Italian bike maker I eventually chose, I wonder if I should have persisted with the Torpado gents a bit more. The Torpado factory in Padua had existed for nearly a century and had sponsored several legendary racers, including Aldo Moser, Cleto Maule as well as Art Longsjo in America via a dealer in Montreal. The Torpado shop was eventually sold and the trademark's new owners closed it sometime in the late 1980s.

At this point I went on a stupid streak. It might be the longest sustained string of bad decisions any business has survived. We went from Torpado in Padua to Milan to find a respected Milanese frame builder. We visited Sante Pogliaghi, whose frames had been ridden to no end of world championships. We found him with a cigarette dangling from his mouth, supervising a couple of young men. One was filing off a giant lump of brass from a seat stay.

Immediately my opinion of Pogliaghi frames fell. But I was here to find Italian frames and so I asked the famous man if he would entertain an order. He laughed. Excusing himself, he left and returned with a clipboard with his orders. Dropping cigarette ash on to the papers, he showed me the ones at the bottom of the pile which would not be shipped for a couple of years. I thanked him for his time and we moved on.

We next talked to Paolo Guerciotti. He was extraordinarily polite, friendly and firm. He could do no business with us because he was selling everything he could get to Ten-Speed Drive of Florida, then the dominant American player in high-end bike wholesale.

We ended up at a large shop named Rossignoli Sport and talked to the owner, Walter Rossignoli. He would be happy to provide us with frames.

Why Your Bike Is Made in Asia

We did not know he would just call up a builder and order them, marking them up along the way. Again, I really had no business being in this business. We gave him an order for fifty frames, to be paid using the most expensive method there is, an irrevocable letter of credit. Also, we did not then know one never imported goods without negotiating a discount from the ocean freight company before arranging shipping. Rossignoli took his sweet time making/acquiring the frames and when they finally came, I called several friends to watch me open the crates.

Opening the first wooden crate was one of the worst moments of my life. Somewhere, the wooden crate had been allowed to sit in the rain. Because it was lined with bubble wrap, the frames at the bottom of the case had sat in water during the journey. They had begun to rust. The chrome was ruined. Italian bike builders generally used what is known as "industrial chrome", where the chrome goes directly on the steel. It is porous and very prone to rust. "Decorative chrome", where layers of copper and nickel are laid down before the chrome is applied was rarely used by European frame builders. Gios forks had decorative chrome.

I just sat there, stunned. I had just blown a large part of Carol's life savings on this heartbreaking pile of steel that had turned out to be more expensive than I had planned because of the unreasonable shipping costs, which in my ignorance I had not seen to, as well as the surprising cost of the letter of credit (L.C.).

I separated out the good frames, which it turned out, were the majority of them. I got on the phone and finally found a painter who would blast the rust off the frames and powder-coat them for a reasonable price. I would at least be able to get my capital back after selling the frames at a deep discount.

I wasn't done being dumb. After our trip to Italy, we ordered Everest chains and freewheels. The chains had slots cut in their side plates. I thought they would be popular among the growing cadre of weight freaks looking to lighten their bikes. What they sent us was junk. The chains shifted very poorly, even by the low standards set by Regina. No one wanted them.

Wait, there's more! After buying a few complete component groups made by the Italian firm Galli, I tracked down their American agent. Given Galli's pricing, I thought this would be a fine alternative to Campagnolo. There is always a serious minority of riders who do not want Campagnolo or the other major brands. I not only ordered a stack of Galli groups, I felt so confident that I placed two more orders to be shipped several months apart.

McGann

Just as they arrived, a Midwest importer who had bypassed the American agent began bringing in Galli and selling the groups for about what I had paid for them. The real meaning of "Herewith we give you our best offer" began to dawn on me. This isn't the best offer, it's the starting point to begin negotiating. More often than not, the eventual long-term success an importer might have with an Italian maker's particular goods was not important to the maker. Each deal was structured with the goal of extracting the maximum amount of money for the manufacturer for a given parcel of goods.

We tried placing a few ads in racing magazines and got absolutely no response. It turned out wholesale wasn't just importing a few items, placing some ads, mailing a price list and waiting for the phone to ring. Everyone else's job usually looks easy. It rarely is.

I had a catastrophe of the first water on my hands. I had spent a huge amount of money on what I had come to view as overpriced junk. As I shook off my gloom, I began to realize it wasn't really junk. The frames were good riding, hand-made Italian frames, the Galli groups worked just fine and the Everest chains and freewheels were also quite usable. What I had done was overpay for goods that had little demand in the American market.

The solution was to take my lumps, give each item a deep markdown and then try again. The knowledge that I had taken our nest egg and squandered it in a poorly thought-out plan steeled me. I absolutely had to succeed in at least getting back to where we started. Luckily, we had a successful bike shop which kept us fed while we learned our new trade.

When we first started the import company, we called it PBC Distributors (PBC standing for Pro Bike Components), but soon realized we needed a real name. High-end buyers were in love with Italy's art-bikes, so we dove into the index of Will and Ariel Durant's *The Renaissance*. We made a list of all the nice-looking and -sounding family and location names and surfaced with Torelli, a fourteenth-century family better-known for its women who married famous men. We needed the name to not only sound good, we wanted to avoid things that would give English-speakers trouble, such as the "ch" sound in Cinelli. It also had to be amenable to good graphic design and fit on the downtube of a frame. A commercial-artist friend approved our choice. We had had enough trouble with product names and actually learned this lesson.

Now knowing that just sending out a mailer wasn't a successful marketing plan, I gassed up Carol's VW Scirocco and started visiting retail shops. Before each sales trip we'd plan which shops I'd visit, Carol would

Why Your Bike Is Made in Asia

sit down with Thomas Guide maps and make an itinerary. They were so detailed, she noted where I would turn right or left as I negotiated the mean streets of Los Angeles (no cell phones with GPS instructions in those days!).

During my first sales calls I would stand around for what seemed interminable waits until a shop's buyer would give me a few moments before dismissing me. But I was determined. And with each visit, I brought an improved product mix as we learned what worked and what didn't. I ended up with a route that stretched 500 miles, from San Diego to Sacramento. For some reason, I really clicked with the shops of California's central valley. I still look back with real pleasure on driving up Route 99, listening to books on tape and visiting solid, kindly bike shop owners.

Late in 1981 everything changed for us. The Italian Trade Commission held a small exhibition in Los Angeles for Italian companies in the bike trade. We arrived late in the afternoon of the final day and had the show almost to ourselves. I got the sense that the show had not been very well attended. Some exhibitors were already starting to take down their booths. As we wandered around the room looking at the displays, there didn't seem to be anyone or anything there that would be a good fit until we came to the final booth.

Standing quietly in front of that booth was a muscular, stocky man who looked about sixty. A slender young lady stood next to him. The booth contained only two bikes. Since we spoke no Italian and they spoke no English, an interpreter was located. We found we were talking to retired pro racer Marcello Faggin and his daughter Cristina. In bike racing, the Faggin name carries weight. I asked Marcello if he knew the late Leandro Faggin, multiple world champion and Olympic gold medalist, who died in 1970 when he was just thirty-seven. "Il mio cugino" [my cousin], he said. These were indeed bike people.

We talked for a while as I looked at the Faggin price list. I asked for a calculator, because the products were priced in Italian Lire, the Euro being decades away. I had to do the currency conversion calculation several times because I was sure I was making a mistake. These were incredible prices, something must be wrong. Yet, the frames were workmanlike with no gaps in the brazing and the paint was tolerably good. This looked to be fine product that in fact, was being sold at a very good price. I said just that to Marcello.

Then, Marcello did the unexpected. "Do you like these bikes?" he asked. I said I did indeed and would contact him later and order some samples.

"Take these two bikes home with you and wire me payment."

"But you don't know me and these bikes are worth a lot of money!"

McGann

"You'll pay me, I am sure of it."

It has been my experience that honest people trust others. This was a good start. A cynic might say that the show was about over, he had clearly made no sales and he might as well try to salvage something from the expensive trip. After all these decades, I think he saw the hook was sunk and we would probably do business.

What we packed into Carol's Scirocco that afternoon were a pair of Campagnolo-equipped bikes. The good one was a real pro bike, made with Columbus SL (then the Italian tubing maker's best) with Nuovo Record parts. The other was a Tre Tubi (three main tubes Columbus SL) with a Campagnolo Gran Sport kit. Both were pantographed—that is, the stem, seat post, crank arms and chain rings were engraved with the Faggin name and logo—then painted in to make a spectacular, special piece of the bicycle builder's art.

Back home in Camarillo, I rode the bikes as did my mechanic and several enthusiasts whose judgement I valued. The verdict was unanimous. These were great-riding bikes at an astounding price. Of course we wired payment for the samples to Faggin. And, we placed an order via Telex (a system of connected teleprinters), faxes and email being years away.

Faggin was in Padua (Padova in Italian), just forty kilometers west of Venice, in the Italian region of Veneto. Generally, builders in the Veneto region were hard-nosed, practical businessmen who produced lower-cost bikes without the expensive finish work that builders from the area around Milan (called Lombardy) perform. Legendary builders Cino Cinelli (though he was originally from Tuscany) and Faliero Masi were the classic Lombard builders, famous for their exquisite finish.

Faggin frameset

Why Your Bike Is Made in Asia

But I had found the right man with the right product for our company. The Faggin frames were soon racing out the door. Very quickly we were selling 1,000 frames a year.

We made other good product choices that fall, spokes from Alpina (later to be replaced by Swiss DT spokes) and d'Alessandro sew-up tires (another brand of tires from the famous Vittoria company). Things were actually starting to click.

Note that, although Asian producers had conquered the consumer market niche, enthusiasts and racers still wanted European bikes. An Italian frame with a Shimano group, however, was not uncommon. Shimano had largely overcome the general resistance to Asian pro bike components.

Finally grasping what would sell, we pressed on.

Before the 1990s, the European bicycle trade show system was very efficient. The Cologne, Germany, show (called "Ifma") was held in even-numbered years in September and the Milan Show (called "Eicma") was held in odd-numbered years in late November. Each year one could see a giant portion of what Europe had to offer at one show in a couple of days. The Cologne show emphasized bikes from the big manufacturers and was dominated by French, German and other northern European companies. The really big Italian companies also came to Cologne. The small specialty Italian builders could afford to show at Milan, given that it was only every other year and close by. We didn't know how good we had it.

Then a new show, Eurobike, in Friedrichshafen, Germany debuted in 1991. It emphasized mountain bikes at a time when they absolutely dominated the world bike market. It was an instant hit. Because Eurobike was held every year, the other shows were forced to defend their turf and also went to a yearly schedule. On top of that, there were the regional Salzburg and London shows at almost the same time. Plus the ever-changing American bike shows could not be ignored. That was chaos. A buyer or exhibitor had to choose his shows carefully, understanding that if he visited or exhibited at just one show, he would miss a lot.

A European manufacturer now had to exhibit at three or more shows to see the same number of customers he used to see at one.

In late 1982 I ran into the same Schwinn sales rep who had laughed at my ambition to open a bike shop. I told him I was beginning to import Italian frames.

"Har! Another line of Brand X bikes coming into the country."

I have to give the man credit. While Schwinn was nearly bankrupt and importing bikes from Asia, hand-made Italian racing bikes were still Brand X in Schwinn World.

1982 was the year Torelli really arrived, but not without hitting a few speed bumps along the way. We started importing Ambrosio rims, though at that time the Italian rim maker had trouble making a smooth joint where the ends of the aluminum extrusion met. We ordered the firm's 2,000-rim minimum (again, at least that was what we were told, but it later turned out to be another opening negotiating volley) and that first order took a while to sell, even at a steep discount. They had poor rim joints that could be felt as the rider braked, making them impossible to sell profitably. At the time French rim maker Mavic made a vastly superior product.

Mavic was a European company that, though it went through difficulties, survived the modern era and its ferocious world-wide competition.

Indicative of how well Mavic was managed in years past, by 1978 the firm was making about 4,000 rims a day and held what was said to be an estimated 65 percent of the world enthusiast rim market, though I find that percentage optimistically high. Mavic wasn't content with just rims.

In 1977 Mavic began making superb bottom brackets and sealed-bearing hubs. Over the next few years Mavic would continue to expand its line, eventually making bars, stems and nearly all the components of a road groupset.

This market dominance resulting from superb product that was well-marketed didn't just magically happen. With the death of Mavic owner Henri Gormand in 1963, the firm suffered from both a war of succession between Gormand's children and terrible financial losses. Son Bruno ended up with money-losing Mavic while his brother ended up with the family's more profitable EMR (Rhône Metallurgical Establishments) firm. EMR was bought by the owners of the Rigida rim company and Rigida was then purchased by Wolber, which finally ended up owned by...Mavic. But I am getting ahead of things.

Bruno set to turning Mavic around. He did so magnificently. In the past, the firm he took over never had more than fifty employees. A combination of improved product and excellent marketing made Mavic the go-to rim brand.

In 1972 Gormand lent his car to a team director sportif at the 1972 Critérium du Dauphiné Libéré (a week-long professional bike race run in southeast France) whose own car had broken down. This allowed the director to continue following the race. That led to Mavic's creating its free

Why Your Bike Is Made in Asia

neutral assistance program with its distinctive yellow cars that followed races with mechanics and equipment to help riders who have mechanical difficulties. It gave Mavic incredible world-wide visibility. Every televised race became an ad for Mavic beginning with the first race Mavic serviced, the 1973 Paris–Nice.

In 1985 Mavic owner Bruno Gormand was killed in a car accident. One would have thought that with the loss of its driven, capable owner the firm would suffer. Not so. Bruno's wife Cécile Gormand was just as capable and led the firm with fire and drive. Mavic thrived.

Indicative of the firm's ceaseless striving, the year after Cécile took over Mavic got its first CAD-CAM design system and not long after introduced the iconic Open 4 CD clincher rim. When the Open 4 CDs first showed up in our warehouse in 1988 they sold as fast as we could get them.

In 1989 Mavic received an unexpected, yet priceless gift. 1986 Tour de France winner Greg LeMond was badly wounded in a hunting accident in 1987. After that near-fatal accident, the American racer's career should have been over. But it wasn't. He slowly regained his competitive strength. In June of 1989 he rode Italy's equivalent of the Tour de France, the Giro d'Italia, and in the final stage of that three-week race, an individual 54-kilometer race against the clock, LeMond was second. He was back.

Two months later in 1989's Tour de France he had a ferocious brawl with Frenchman Laurent Fignon, who had won the Tour in 1983 and 1984. With just one stage to go Fignon led LeMond by just fifty seconds. In the incredible final stage of that Tour LeMond beat Fignon by fifty-eight seconds, winning the Tour by just eight seconds. Perhaps the most exciting race in cycling history was won by a man who should have been dead, and he did it on a Mavic-equipped bike.

LeMond wasn't done yet. Late in August he won the World Road Championships for a second time. I hope Mavic management went to church to thank a munificent God. No one could have thought equipping LeMond's lower-ranked ADR cycling team would yield such an incredible result. In 1989 both the Yellow and Rainbow jerseys were won on Mavic-equipped bikes.

Wait, there's more. That same year, French racing great Jeannie Longo won the Women's Tour de France riding a Mavic-equipped bike.

That year our wholesale catalogue devoted more space to Mavic equipment than to Campagnolo.

In 1990, a group of four Mavic executives who had been with the firm since the 1970s bought the company from Madame Gormand. One of the quartet, Jean-Pierre Lacomb became the firm's manager and under his guidance Mavic tried to take bike components in a new direction.

Not everything Mavic tried worked. In 1992 Mavic introduced its ZAP group with an innovative set of electronic gear changers. I believe ZAP was the first production electronic gear shifting system. Though to this day it has ferocious advocates, it wasn't reliable enough (especially on rainy days) for general commercial sale and it was quickly withdrawn from the market. Mavic did not give up on electronic shifting and in 1999 it came out with its wireless Mektronic system. It too had to be pulled from the market after reliability problems emerged.

In 1993 Torelli took a tolerable hit. Though he had long-denied having such plans because he wanted to keep the product flowing, the American manager of Mavic USA had decided to discontinue selling Mavic to distributors and sell directly to bike shops. We were more or less ready for this and were not surprised. Rumors had been in the air for months.

Fortunately, by this time we were bringing in Italian rims branded Torelli, which is what we should have been doing all along. After trying to grey-market (import from a European Mavic distributor without Mavic's permission) Mavic rims for a short time, we closed out the line and concentrated on our own rims.

Mavic was not done being bought and sold. In 1994 the Mavic executives sold the firm to the Salomon group, most famous for its production of ski equipment.

In 1998 Salomon merged with Adidas to form Adidas-Salomon, the second largest sporting goods company in the world. In 2018 Salomon spun off Mavic to an American investment group.

By this point Mavic presented a problem to its owners and distributors, as the high-end products the market was looking for were not being produced by Mavic. The firm could not competitively make the carbon rims, disc wheels, and other parts that performance customers wanted.

Astonishingly, the prestigious firm that had dominated the rim marketplace in the 1980s and 1990s went into receivership on May 2, 2020. After the smoke had cleared, French courts supervised the acquisition of Mavic by the French Bourrelier group. Out of the 210 Mavic employees still remaining, the reorganization saved the jobs of 107. How this smaller Mavic will do in this increasingly competitive world is yet to be seen. But in 2021 Mavic increased its sales by 20 percent and hired fifty-seven new workers. Though Mavic has done better than many European bike component manufacturers, its dominance is long gone and this writer doesn't see how that market ownership can ever be regained.

Why Your Bike Is Made in Asia

There was another historic break in all this financial turbulence. In 2021 Mavic lost the right to run its famed neutral support at races run by the ASO organization, most notably, the Tour de France and Paris–Roubaix. And who runs that service as of this writing in 2024? Shimano.

As we grew, our now twelve-page catalog gained some depth with Selle Royal saddles, tubulars with the Vittoria name, and Reg accessories, among others.

Earlier I had mentioned the legendary Cino Cinelli. Though the bulk of his business was in bars and stems, he still continued to produce a limited number of bikes, such as those Supercorsas I had bought from Mike Sinyard for the retail shop years before. Cinelli's agent in the U.S. mentioned to me that there was some production capacity (I assume that meant a Cinelli subcontractor was looking for orders) and knew I wanted to do a high-end Torelli bike or frame. We ordered a few frames from Cinelli made with our graphics and the results were simply stunning. They were beautiful and rode as well as they looked. They were expensive, so we didn't sell many, but we felt real pride as each one left our warehouse.

At what I believe was the 1984 Cologne show we met the S.J. Clarks Cables people. The Birmingham, England, firm made brake and gear cables and brake housing of the finest quality. I had purchased products made by Clarks from United Cycle Supply for my shop and knew the British company made a first-rate product. Moreover, everyone we dealt with at the show and thereafter was kind and knowledgeable. We placed an order and Clarks Cables became a core product for us from the day we received our first shipment. We didn't discontinue Clarks until the early 2000s, when the firm was sold.

Clarks was a joy to work with. During one visit to their factory we saw machinery producing 1,000-foot rolls of housing for bike factories. This was before indexing and compression-free housing. It was simply flat-wire wound housing coated with plastic. That was what was usually used for both brakes and gears before 1990 and the introduction of indexed shifting. To reduce friction between the wire and the housing, a plastic liner could be inserted into the housing and we sold rolls of that liner to go with the housing. But, the necessary gap between the housing and the liner caused brakes to feel mushy. Still, we thought bike shops would love to get the big rolls for their workrooms. They would always have a ready supply and the housing's cost-per-foot was incredibly low.

We imported a few rolls of housing and liner and sold them very quickly. We re-ordered and continued to sell them for years.

In 1989 Clarks developed machinery that eliminated that problem of mushy feeling brakes. The flat wire of the housing was physically wrapped around the liner, preventing movement of the liner within the housing. This new housing from Clarks, called Autolined, gave brakes and gears a crisp and firm feel.

It wasn't until 1995 that Clarks finally idled the machinery that produced the traditional unlined housing. The industry had moved on to better things.

Though we were the exclusive U.S. distributor of Clarks bicycle products, we had learned that one's exclusivity was highly dependent on both the distributor's willingness to honor that agreement as well as distributors in other countries respecting the territories the manufacturer has established. Wanting to both guard ourselves against another Alvarez—who had grey-marketed product into the U.S. for which we thought we had an exclusive, but more on this later—and use our trademarked Torelli name for the wires and housing, we asked Clarks to ship our orders in Torelli packaging. That gave us one less product name to promote. Good guys that they were, they immediately agreed.

This move served us well when after the Clarks family sold the firm we were able to simply move our production to Asia, where we were able to widen our range of cables and housing and get improved product to boot. For example. We could now offer die-drawn, super smooth stainless steel wires, coated with PTFE for even less friction.

Though we had moved our own cable buying to Asia, not long after Clarks also set up manufacturing in China and soon had offices in both Taiwan and China and offered a hugely expanded product line. Clarks boss Tony Wright was quoted in 2013 by the British business website BusinessLive saying, "All bikes are made in Asia nowadays and by acting as an original equipment manufacturer in China, we are generating our own aftermarket." In a single sentence Mr. Wright summed up much of what this book is about.

While the U.S. market had largely (there were some notable exceptions such as Peugeot, but the clock was ticking) moved to Asian bikes, I sensed an opening in talking to my customers. The dollar was strong and there was real prestige in almost everything Italian. With that in mind we went to the 1983 Milan show to see if we could have a complete bike made that would retail for about $400. I still dreamed of selling a Euro-made complete bike.

I succeeded beyond my wildest dreams. The Vicini shop, located near the Adriatic coast in Cesena, had been started by legendary racer Mario Vicini. We talked to his younger son Ottavio about my plan (the older son, also named Mario, had feuded with the family and started his own shop, SAB, in San Marino).

Why Your Bike Is Made in Asia

I knew the Italians could make a light bike that used less expensive components from prestigious makers. We ended up with a 22-pound bike equipped with Campagnolo 990 derailleurs, Modolo brakes, Ofmega cranks, and Michelin's new Bib tires. It wasn't as rugged as the Japanese equivalent, but it rode beautifully and was pounds lighter than other bikes that retailed for our opening price of just $369.

I ordered a 20-foot container, holding 150 complete bikes, and waited. Well, I didn't just sit around. I had a sample of what we named the Torelli Corsa Strada and took it to my customers. Long before the container arrived, the complete shipment was sold out. It was the right bike at the right time.

But… the bike came with the new state-of-the art Michelin Bib tires made with a smooth tread. I think, by sheer accident, I was the first to bring in these wonderful tires to the U.S. I had talked to the Michelin people and they said all their research about handling and cornering showed that, given a high-pressure bicycle road tire's small contact patch, the tread pattern did not improve the tires' road grip. In fact, tread degraded the grip (even in the rain) and slowed the bike. If Michelin doesn't know about tires, who does? I did get a few of what I knew were inevitable phone calls. Some bike shops and retail customers were aghast at the smooth tires and many cared not a whit about Michelin's research. I was happy to trade the smooth tires for ones from Asia with tread. One does not win fights with customers.

I ordered another can of Corsa Stradas. It too sold out before it arrived.

The bike business is a small community and in the end everyone knows everything about everyone's business. My Corsa Strada niche was small. After a couple of other importers brought in bikes similar to the Corsa Strada, sales came more slowly. And, to put it kindly, my supplier grew more and more difficult to deal with. We were forced to abandon the project in 1988.

We got over the hiccup of the first Ambrosio rim shipment and began importing the firm's handlebar tape, Bike Ribbon. I have no idea how many thousands of packages of Bike Ribbon we sold, but it seemed every order left with some. Over time we became very good friends with the Marzorati family that owned Ambrosio, particularly the third-generation manager of the firm, Marzio. Marzio understood the modern marketplace and its pressures, he worked tirelessly to improve his company's products. He ended up with rims and wheels that exhibited all the care and beauty that made Lombard bike products famous. Sadly, a sudden illness took the too-young Marzio in 2009.

Back to the BMX business: In 1984 I had ordered a new model of RedLine BMX bicycle for my bike shop, the 500a. It offered superb specifications plus the cherished RedLine name, for about $200 retail. Upon receiving my first shipment I was astonished to see it was made not in Japan, but in Taiwan—as far as I was concerned, the source of almost nothing but junk bikes.

In 1974, Taiwan had 150 bicycle factories making more than two million bicycles and exporting the majority of them. The crash of the bike boom hit Taiwan's bike makers hard, with sales down to little more than a third of what it had been. Moreover, along with King Liu's initiating higher production standards, the government instituted an inspection program to keep low-quality bikes from being exported. By 1976 there were just thirty-seven Taiwan bike makers.

I had been asleep. Though somewhat aware of KHS, I had no idea of the extent of Taiwan's share of the quality bike market. Since 1977, Giant Bicycles of Taiwan had been producing bikes for Schwinn, and during the 1980 United Auto Workers strike that shut down Schwinn's Chicago production (Schwinn's factory employees belonged to the UAW), Giant had the ability to send Schwinn 200,000 bikes a year. The bikes were more than acceptable. In 1982 Giant began producing Schwinn's first competitive BMX bike, the Predator, which was a solid hit.

RedLine owner Linn Kasten had been under pressure from his distributors to trade down-market. To hit the $200.00 retail price point, Kasten had to move his production from Kawamura in Japan to Giant to take advantage of Taiwan's lower costs.

One of the obstacles to making high-end BMX bikes was the shortage of highly skilled welders who could join the lightweight steel tubes. To get around this, Giant had installed pulsed TIG machines which cost more initially, but were cheaper and easier to run, although they had to use thicker-walled and therefore heavier tubing. The resultant welds still looked good, even if not as fine as the artful TIG welds coming from the United States and Japan, and they were plenty strong.

The 500a was the first Taiwanese bike I was proud to sell in my retail shop. The frame welds were excellent and the components, all made in Taiwan, had superb fit and finish. The bike went together easily and didn't return to the shop with problems. Taiwan had truly arrived.

At Torelli Imports, things were going well. The Faggins were selling, but Cinelli as a private-label frame supplier wasn't really a good match. We went to the 1985 Milan bike show with the specific purpose of finding a high-end frame to complement the Faggins. As we wandered the giant, noisy hall, one frame stood out. It was simply beautiful: gorgeous candy-apple red paint had been applied to a frame of superb workmanship. Yet, it

Why Your Bike Is Made in Asia

was a name I didn't know, Mondonico. Moreover, it was in the Guerciotti booth. Years ago I had been completely rebuffed by Paolo Guerciotti because the largest pro bike wholesaler in the country, Ten Speed Drive Imports (TSDI), had been burying him with orders. Ten Speed Drive was doing so well, it opened a second warehouse in Carpenteria, California, to complement its Florida headquarters.

Yet, now Paolo wanted to talk. I was surprised to find that he knew about us and our place in the American market. Paolo paid attention to business and his success was no accident. He was smart and worked like a dog. He said nothing bad about TSDI, which in fact was starting to exhibit the earliest signs of financial difficulty (it would fold around 1991), but clearly Paolo wanted to widen his customer base. Earlier, looking for a reliable quality builder to make his Guerciotti bikes, Paolo had partnered with Antonio Mondonico. The two had set up a framebuilding shop in Mondonico's hometown, Concorezzo, a suburb of Milan.

Mondonico at the time was busy building Guerciotti bikes. He was at first reluctant to let us, a comparatively small distributor compared to TSDI, be his exclusive American distributor. Though Guerciotti really wanted Mondonico to deal with us, we had to talk with Antonio at length and visit his workshop. Eventually we had a deal. The first Mondonico frames arrived in 1986. We now had two superb builders supplying us with frames: Faggin in Veneto, for the price conscious, and Lombard builder Mondonico for the rider looking for the *ne plus ultra*, the very best.

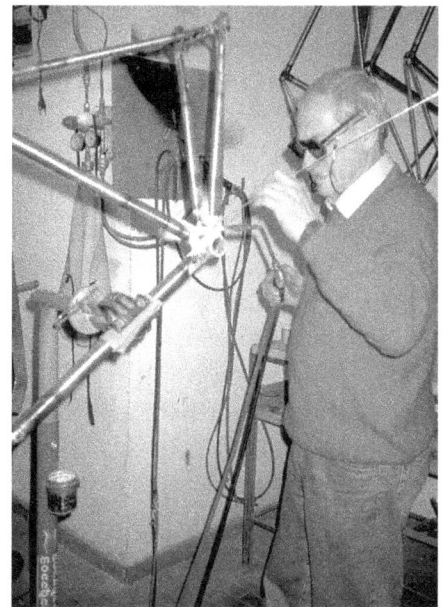

Antonio Mondonico, master craftsman, at his task

McGann

We got another benefit from the agreement. Guerciotti did a booming business as a trading agent. He stocked a huge inventory of Italian product, including Campagnolo, for both domestic wholesale and for sale to his international customers. Moreover, he could use his buying muscle to place orders with factories as an agent and get competitive prices for importers. Even after Mondonico and Guerciotti ended their partnership in 1989, we remained close to the Guerciottis for years.

Now we were really cooking.

There was an elephant in the room that so far has not been mentioned. Remember those BMX boys who transformed their 20-inch bikes into formidable dirt bikes and spawned an industry to make them? There was a parallel movement involving adult 26-inch wheel bikes.

In the mid-1970s a group of friends in Northern California started descending Mount Tamalpais on balloon-tired, coaster-brake bikes. They got so good at it that after a single descent, the now hot, dry rear hub brake would have to be disassembled and re-greased because so much heat had been generated on the insane ride down the mountain. The challenging route was named "Repack" for the rear-hub rebuild that had to be done after the descent. It seems that from the start, these bikes, mounted with wider, reinforced handlebars, were called "mountain bikes". Very quickly these mountain bike riders wanted higher-performance machines than the ancient Schwinns they were converting.

Historian Jobst Brandt dates the first quality mountain bikes, handmade in northern California (of course) from lightweight tubing, to late 1977. By then mountain bikes had drum brakes, SunTour derailleurs, TA cotterless cranks and motorcycle brake levers.

Things were moving fast. Famed racer and frame builder Tom Ritchey made a few custom mountain bikes. But it was Gary Fisher's and Joe Breeze's bikes that might be the first popular production (though limited) mountain bikes.

Mike Sinyard had already imported complete Japanese bikes: a racing model called Allez and a touring bike named Sequoia. As usual, Sinyard had nailed the timing, specs and pricing. In my shop Specialized road bikes were instantly in demand.

With the growth of mountain biking starting in northern California right under Sinyard's nose, it was no surprise that in 1981 Specialized introduced the Stumpjumper. It was probably the first production mountain bike and was a giant hit, and again, rightly so.

Mountain bikes used more upright bars, making the position far more comfortable than on a drop-bar road bike. To get up steep dirt roads, they

Why Your Bike Is Made in Asia

came with an enormous gear range, including extremely low gears. Fat tires with knobby treads that could take rough dirt roads were absolutely necessary. That had the extra benefit of giving a more comfortable ride than the skinny high-pressure tires on high-performance road bikes. And mountain bikes were tough, built to take hard treatment on dirt trails. They were reliable and comfortable. That's what people really wanted.

Almost overnight the bike industry changed. Every bike company realized that if they didn't have mountain bikes, and fast, their dealers would go elsewhere. The Japanese and Taiwanese responded quickly. A vast quantity of mountain bikes, at all price ranges and qualities, flooded the market. While the early mountain bikes had used some European components, particularly the French T.A. Cyclotouriste triple crankset, there was no great rush on the part of European component makers to produce mountain-specific parts. That European inertia had tragic consequences for the continental parts makers. The Japanese soon dominated the marketplace with well-designed mountain-specific parts. By the mid-1980s Asian makers owned this now-vital part of the business.

Oh, and in the late 1970s Schwinn sent several engineers to see what Gary Fisher was up to. They looked at his odd-looking (by the standards of the time) mountain bike and expressed contempt for what they thought was an amateurish product. As it had with the first BMX bikes, Schwinn had failed to recognize another coming bicycle revolution.

The result of the Asians seizing the reins of mountain bike production? Yet more bike shop floor space was taken by well-made Asian-produced bikes.

8
Twelve years after

Let's see where the world bicycle industry stood in 1986. It was very different from than the one I stumbled into in 1974. Those twelve years had seen astonishing transformations.

First of all, BMX and mountain bikes were new and important additions to the product mix. Second, in late 1985 the governments of France, West Germany, Japan, Great Britain and the United States entered into an agreement to work together to intervene in world currency markets to devalue the then very strong U.S. Dollar. The Plaza Accord was the result of a vigorous campaign by American manufacturers who found the strong Dollar of the early 1980s made their goods too expensive to export. And at the same time, imported goods were extraordinarily cheap.

The market intervention was successful. The Dollar plummeted sharply, more than 50 percent against the Japanese Yen between 1985 and 1987. To stop the Dollar's scary-fast fall, another agreement, called the Louvre Accord, was signed in early 1987. Slowly, the Dollar partially rebounded, though this might have been more through the increase in American interest rates that made Dollar investments more lucrative than because of the Louvre Accord.

This was a difficult time for American importers. During the steepest decline of the Dollar against the Yen, my bike shop was getting new price lists from Western States almost weekly as they tried to price their stock to cover their replacement costs. Whenever inflation is severe, people not in business argue fiercely against merchants raising the prices of their current inventory, saying the goods should be sold according to their acquisition cost, not their replacement cost. A quick thought experiment will show that soon a businessman would be out of stock as his selling price wouldn't cover his expenses and the cost of replacement inventory.

And with our usual perfect timing, we sold our retail store to concentrate on building up Torelli Imports.

In late 1984 Shimano finally delivered what had been an obvious company goal, reliable indexed shifting. Before indexed shifting, with but few exceptions, shift levers were usually kept in place with some form of friction washers. A rider had to acquire a bit of skill to move the chain from one cog to another. It could be especially difficult when maneuvering the chain across the smaller rear sprockets where the derailleur's jockey wheel was farthest from the cog, though SunTour's slant parallelogram derailleurs had vastly improved friction shifting. Now, with Shimano's SIS indexed shifting, the rider could feel a detent or "click" in the lever and each detent corresponded with a cog in the rear cluster. Suddenly anyone could make accurate and fast shifts.

Easier shifting had long been an important part of Shimano design. The firm made several attempts to address this seemingly simple but actually extraordinarily complex problem. Back in 1975 Shimano introduced the "Positron" system which used two rigid wires to actuate a rear derailleur with detents. In this attempt at indexed shifting, the detents were in the derailleur. Soon the Positron was simplified to a single wire and it worked well enough to be equipment on less-expensive consumer bikes sold in specialty bike stores. I sold a few in my shop. But no one was knocking down the doors to get a Positron bike.

Shimano kept at it, constantly improving every aspect of the drive train, including chain, rear cog and front chainring design. And of course, derailleurs received serious attention.

Those SIS bikes Shimano showed in 1984 used a complete shifting system. The entire gear train was proprietary. An integrated, complete system was necessary to make the shifting both dependable and easy. The detents were now in the levers, but if the rider needed to change wheels (and thus use a freewheel not exactly positioned for the indexed shifting on his bike) or simply preferred not to use the indexing, it was a simple matter to switch the levers to the friction shifting mode.

The gear wires were pre-stretched so that changing wire tension as the lever was pulled would not change its length, and hence where the derailleur would end up at a particular place in its arc and thus reliably deliver a shift.

Until this point, gear housing was a wound helical coil covered with plastic. Under load the housing would compress, death to accurate indexed shifting. Even Clarks autolined housing compressed slightly. SIS gear housing uses compression-free longitudinal wires that run the length of the

Why Your Bike Is Made in Asia

housing. The magnitude of the challenge of making indexed shifting work can be seen in what it took so that a specific amount of cable movement at the lever resulted in the same movement at the derailleur.

The chainrings and rear cogs now had profiles that allowed the chain to fall easily in place. Even after the SIS introduction Shimano constantly improved this aspect of its system.

And the rear derailleur. Shimano had been waiting for the SunTour slant parallelogram patent to expire. Now, with the derailleur sprung at the top (with a precisely calculated tension) and a slant parallelogram, the jockey wheel would always be at the optimal distance from the freewheel cog. This complete system, subtle in its myriad details and truly impressive as a total package, was an extraordinary advance in the state of the art.

Shimano made a brilliant marketing move by initially making the system available only in their top-end Dura-Ace group, giving the indexing system real prestige. And if there were any questions about the system's racing competitiveness, Andy Hampsten put those to rest when he became the first American to win the three-week Giro d'Italia in 1988 and he did it on a Shimano Dura-Ace SIS equipped bike.

Andy Hampsten in bad weather in the 1988 Giro d'Italia. Photo by Fotoreporter Sirotti.

SunTour, a much smaller company, was competing for the same OEM (original equipment manufacturer) business that Shimano was capturing. The constant stream of Shimano innovations during mid-to-late 1980s as well as Shimano's growing range of components put the smaller component maker on the ropes.

SunTour had supplied nearly half the derailleurs on bikes American bike shops sold in the earlier 1980s. Though SunTour had responded reasonably quickly in 1987 (two years after Shimano's SIS) with its own indexed system, Accushift, it wasn't the sophisticated complete system Shimano was selling. It did not shift nearly as well, making life still more difficult for the company that had once dominated its market. By the early 1990s, crushed by Shimano and Taiwanese competition as well as the upward revaluation of the Yen, SunTour had a minuscule portion of the market and in 1994 SunTour closed its Japanese factory. A year later the company was sold to a Taiwan group, and the company that had dominated the derailleur market for years ceased to exist.

Shimano was converting its factories to SARA—Shimano Automated Robotic Assembly—making its factories ever more efficient, driving down its per-unit costs, and making its competitors' lives even more miserable.

The Yen revaluation didn't just hit SunTour. The bike companies who were producing many of the world's bikes, such as Kawamura, suddenly found their customers running to Taiwan.

This was a tough business.

In France, slow-to-change Peugeot didn't quite stand still. The company's most advanced bike, the PY10FC, used a carbon/aluminum frame made by the French Vitus firm. Materials other than steel were starting to take hold, even at Peugeot.

The rest of the Peugeot line used steel frames, but even in the fabrication of steel frames, there were real changes. Peugeot had abandoned lugs. Its steel frames were now lugless-brazed, made with advanced automatic machinery.

And those execrable plastic derailleurs and steel cottered cranksets? Gone. Even the commuter bikes with fenders and racks had cotterless cranks and good side-pull brakes. Simplex had abandoned Delrin and had gone back to making decent derailleurs. The rear derailleurs were not unlike Shimano Crane changers of the era, sprung top and bottom with a SunTour parallelogram tilt. But they were friction systems, not indexed. In other words, the bikes were decent, and now reliable. Yet they were far from cutting edge and still well behind their Asian counterparts.

Simplex finally went bankrupt in 1985 and according to historian Frank Berto the firm that rose from the ashes eventually merged with Italian parts maker Ofmega. Ofmega continued to produce Simplex branded derailleurs.

Why Your Bike Is Made in Asia

Hammered by declining margins and the increasing costs of maintaining its legendary cycling team, late in 1986 Peugeot announced it would no longer sponsor its own team.

In Italy, Campagnolo's initial response to Shimano's series of brilliant gear innovations was to treat indexed shifting with contempt. SIS was for riders who didn't know how to shift. Campagnolo cemented that message by handing out Halloween "cricket" clickers at a bike show, saying this was for people who needed "click shifting". The company continued to produce exquisitely made, extremely reliable components using decades-old design technology. The fierce customer loyalty Campagnolo had built over the decades by making the finest bicycle parts in the world stood the firm in good stead as they were buffeted by the fierce storm coming from the East.

Finally sobering up and realizing that indexed shifting wasn't going to be laughed away, Campagnolo made its first foray into indexed shifting with a miserable system called Syncro. Since Campagnolo didn't make a slant-parallelogram rear derailleur, nor their own freewheel nor chain, the system used various notched discs (two different discs, I believe, for the first version) that were inserted into newly-designed shift lever that worked the rear derailleur, each positioning the derailleur differently for either 6- or 7-speed. By 1988 there were seven different discs. It couldn't work well. And it didn't.

Campagnolo put out a series of various derailleurs, all designed as if to say that they could make indexed gear systems without the fundamental requirement that the jockey pulley stay a constant distance from the freewheel cog. There were a couple of brilliant attempts to do this workaround. The mid-range (by Campagnolo standards, though still a high-end derailleur) Chorus changer had a slant parallelogram with two positions. The body could be loosened and adjusted to become a wider range derailleur. But because the top mounting bolt was unsprung, the jockey pulley could not maintain a constant distance from the freewheel. Again, because Campagnolo was ignoring one of the fundamental requirements of an indexed derailleur, they (and I) were making and selling product that could not perform the task for which it was intended: accurate, indexed shifting.

And with the 1988 Croce d'Aune changer—named for the frozen pass where it was claimed Tullio Campagnolo came up with the idea for the hub quick-release—Campagnolo again had a brilliant design that would have been a wonderful advancement a few years before. Pulling on the rear derailleur cable pulled the derailleur down and away from the freewheel, actuating a rod that pushed the derailleur inward, towards the larger cogs. The 1988 Campagnolo catalog described it thus: "The 'Twin-Axle System' of the Croce D'Aune derailleur is a new break-through in derailleur technology and is destined to set new standards for competition derailleurs. In races like the Giro d'Italia and Tour de France where steep mountain roads torture both man and machine it is extremely important for the derailleur to perform flawlessly because one missed shift or slipped chain can be the difference between winning and losing." The brilliant but uncompetitive derailleur was soon discontinued.

While Campagnolo was producing bike parts of first-rate workmanship and third-rate design for road riders, the siren call of the exploding mountain bike market attracted the Italian company's attention. A series of groups that no one wanted were produced. Only the most committed Campagnolo fans remember Icarus, Euclid and the other off-road groups. And the less said about Campagnolo BMX, the better. Campagnolo gave up on the off-road market in 1996.

It was in 1991 that Campagnolo finally surrendered on road design, now producing the long delayed double-sprung slant parallelogram rear derailleurs, mated with the rest of an integrated control group.

Campagnolo had run into the bicycle version of Moore's Law which predicted an exponential rate of increasing computer power, which held true from about 1975 to perhaps about 2016. That same increase in the speed of bicycle technological change hit Campagnolo. The Italian company was able to make Nuovo Record rear derailleurs for about sixteen years. By the 1990s, it seemed that every day some aspect of some kind of bicycle was improved.

Yet, Italy was alive with both a thriving consumer-commuter industry as well as a raft of companies producing enthusiast bikes and parts. Northern Italy was covered with small shops like Faggin and Mondonico. And there were component makers besides Campagnolo, including Ofmega (which should be remembered if only for their early 1980s colorful Mistral plastic derailleurs—made in pink, among other colors—that actually worked well, and were reliable, unlike Simplex's product) and Gipiemme.

Gipiemme started as a job shop for other component makers but eventually developed its own component range. Both Ofmega and Gipiemme made good products and I was proud to include their equipment in my catalog. But, like the other Europeans, they (and I) were selling dated merchandise.

Back in the U.S., Schwinn's Chicago factory had been starved of money and resources. It was beat-up, obsolete and run with worn-out tooling that dedicated employees managed to keep repaired. By the late 1970s, Schwinn

Why Your Bike Is Made in Asia

management knew something had to be done. Under the terms of Ignaz' trust, Ed Schwinn, nephew of Frank V. Schwinn, was next in line to become president of the company. He led the effort to relocate to a new factory in Tulsa, Oklahoma. The site was selected. But, the $50 million dollars the move would cost left the Schwinn family gasping for air. In the face of falling sales, the transfer was nixed. The family didn't have the money to build the new plant and the thought of selling a piece of the firm to finance the new factory was a non-starter. Schwinn would stay the private property of the Schwinn family.

Incredibly, the Oklahoma factory was going to be equipped with the same old steel welding technology that was used to make Varsity frames. It would have been obsolete before the first bike was made. It also showed that despite the good sales the welded steel bikes enjoyed during the new-factory planning, the Schwinns still had not come to grips with the necessity of building modern lightweight-bikes with higher-strength steels. This blindness was long-standing. Back in the early 1970s Schwinn dealers had already begun asking about the possibility of getting lighter-weight Schwinns. Crown and Coleman told of a dealer meeting where that question was answered with, "Are you gonna ride it or carry it?"

One consequence of the attempted move was a feeling within the company that Schwinn was quite willing to dump its career employees. The sense that the employees were part of a Schwinn company family had started to break down during the stress of the round-the-clock bike production of the 1970s. Through the years the workers had been represented by an in-house union. Indicative of the growing sense of resentment, in 1980 the employees voted to join the United Auto Workers union. Given the Schwinn family feeling that the entire company was their property to do with as they wished, dealing with the UAW was something they simply did not want to do. As bargaining for improved benefits went nowhere, the union voted to go on strike that September. The strike lasted four months resulting in some small gains for the workers.

To help Schwinn survive the strike, Schwinn's Taiwan supplier Giant Bicycles vastly upped its production, taking enormous risks along the way. Schwinn did not seek other suppliers, and Giant's risk-taking was rewarded.

And what about those BMX boys? For years Schwinn tried to ignore this vital market segment. And when they did finally make a consumer BMX bike, the Scrambler, in 1975, it was with the heavy tubing used on the Sting-Ray. It wasn't until 1983 that Schwinn imported the Predator lightweight BMX bike from Taiwan. The company had not just lost the immediate sales a timely, marketable BMX bike would have brought the firm, Schwinn's failure was far greater than that. The firm had missed creating a whole demographic cohort of boys dreaming of owning a Schwinn who would go on to crave teen and adult Schwinn bikes and pass that desire to own a Schwinn to their children. The long chain of youthful devotion to Schwinn was broken.

Schwinn did finally produce a competitive mountain bike in 1984, but it had to go to Taiwan to have it made with thin-wall, lightweight tubing. Both the Schwinn Chicago factory and its American subcontractor Murray could only fabricate frames in heavy mild steel.

In 1979 Ed Schwinn took over his family's company and set about removing the executives who been running the company for Frank V. One move turned out to have a series of completely unintended consequences. Vice-president Al Fritz, who is credited with getting the Sting-Ray produced, had become a champion of a different kind of exercycle, one that could give the upper body as well as the legs a workout.

Ed Schwinn set up a new company, Excelsior Sports, to produce and sell what was eventually named the Schwinn Airdyne and put an unwilling Fritz in charge of the operation. Ed was effectively kicking Al Fritz upstairs. The product turned out to be the smash success Fritz was certain it would be. Initially it was manufactured domestically, but as with much of Schwinn's product line, Schwinn turned to Taiwan bike maker Giant who was already making bikes for Schwinn, to build the machine. Giant had been going through a very rough patch. Insiders say the bike maker was nearly bankrupt. The profit from making those tens of thousands of exercycles (67,000 in 1986) put Giant over the hump, allowing it to become the powerhouse company it is today.

As for Fritz, who had made so much money for Schwinn during Frank V's tenure and was now running a very successful subsidiary, Ed still wanted him gone. He made it so in 1985, forcing the resistant executive to retire. Fritz was an extraordinary man who had risen to his high management position despite having only an eighth-grade education. He was the last of the old-line Schwinn managers and the company was now being run by Ed and his team.

Ed Schwinn and his staff wanted to have nothing to do with the UAW. The solution Schwinn embraced seemed to be the product of a petulant child. The company did not want to overhaul the run-down, worn-out Chicago factory that was now staffed with an organized workforce. So incredibly, Schwinn built a new factory in Greenville, Mississippi which opened in 1981. There was no good reason to build a bike factory in what

Why Your Bike Is Made in Asia

was a logistical dead end. First, there was no existing good water supply for such a large factory. Being seventy-five miles from the closest interstate, trucking was difficult and expensive, and there was no air transport facility nearby. It was missing all the advantages that had made Chicago such a great place to build bikes.

Indeed, Greenville was a strange place to locate a factory which would depend upon imported components and then need to ship the finished product all over the country. But Mississippi was a right-to-work state, meaning if a company's workers have a union, employees don't have to join, nor pay union dues. That was what mattered to the Schwinns.

Schwinn management tried to run the doomed, expensive Mississippi factory from Chicago. No one wanted to move to Mississippi. The factory, bleeding huge amounts of money the Schwinns could not spare, was shut down in 1991.

Through the early 1980s, more and more of the Chicago bike production was moved to either American builder Murray or overseas, mostly to Giant in Taiwan. Schwinn closed its legendary Chicago factory at the end of 1983.

But, closing the factory and mainly sourcing bikes from overseas saved the firm. By the mid-1980s, Schwinn was enjoying soaring sales and was again profitable, even with the burden of the Mississippi factory. Though the firm was put on a short leash by the banks, infuriating Ed Schwinn, the Schwinn family could feel reasonably comfortable that the company was back on track and had a great future.

Schwinn sold 986,000 bikes in 1986. But the company was not what it once was, a maker of high-quality bikes produced in America's heartland. Instead, Schwinn was primarily an importer with a storied, almost legendary name.

Crucially, by paying Giant to produce most of its bicycles and trainers, Schwinn made two classic business errors. It lost the leverage a canny buyer has when the supplier fears losing a customer's business to other existing suppliers. Schwinn was clearly locked into using Giant as its main bicycle supplier. And, Schwinn turned Giant into a powerful maker of bikes that a few years later was selling "Giant" brand bikes all over the world. Schwinn had created a powerful competitor.

Schwinn made another error. Before helping turn Giant into a monster bike maker, Schwinn did not try to buy a piece of the Taiwan firm. When Schwinn finally sobered up and offered to buy a share of Giant, Giant's boss Tony Lo instead offered to buy a piece of Schwinn.

Stung by that episode, Schwinn looked to the Chinese mainland and in 1987 purchased a one-third (initially reported to be 18 percent) share in

China Bicycles. In 1990 China Bicycles would buy Western States Imports and acquire the valuable Diamondback brand in a complex transaction that left Schwinn without any equity in Western States. But at the time China Bicycles could neither match Giant's quality nor produce the quantity of bikes Ed Schwinn wanted. After upsetting Giant's Tony Lo, Ed Schwinn came back to him 1991 needing to increase his purchases of Giant-made bikes. One can't help thinking the Dunning-Kruger Effect was in play here: a cognitive bias in which a person of low ability in an area, such as running a bicycle company, over-estimates his capability in that enterprise.

Ed Schwinn wasn't done. In 1988, with the Mississippi factory still causing Schwinn to bleed large amounts of precious cash, he bought a 41.1 percent share in then Iron-Curtain Hungary's Csepel Works with dreams of using its production to gain a foothold in the European market. The ancient factory was in worse condition than the Schwinn Chicago factory in its final days. The cost? $958,000. Schwinn then made a considerable investment in modernizing the factory so that it could turn out marketable bikes, which it did for Schwinn for years.

As Schwinn's problems multiplied, with bikes coming from various factories, some with dubious or outdated finishes, and deliveries getting ever more unreliable, dealers started taking on other brands, especially Trek and Specialized. This made Schwinn's management crazy. There didn't seem to be a collective wondering why these dealers, many of them second-generation top producers, were going elsewhere for product, nor were there signs of some much-needed needed introspection. Schwinn should have been looking for ways to make these dealers, incredibly valuable assets to the firm, happy.

Instead, Schwinn set out to punish a few to make examples of them by revoking their Schwinn franchises. To this writer and lifetime merchant, it seemed the worst possible strategy.

By this time Trek was a $30-million company. In 1984 the firm made 60,000 bikes. Though earlier it had hit a rough patch and had tried to sell itself to Schwinn and Specialized, company boss Richard Burke streamlined the company and put it on a profitable basis. From here on it went from strength to strength.

An interesting shifter set was introduced in 1988. The SRAM Grip Shift was originally created to fit on the end of aerodynamic triathlon time-trial bars so that the rider could shift without taking his hands off the bars. Few could have predicted how far the firm (with a name taken from letters in the founders' first names) with its twist-grip shifters would go.

Why Your Bike Is Made in Asia

Quickly both the Grip Shift makers and riders realized that the shifters had a far wider set of applications, including on mountain bikes, and on the ends of the drops of road bikes. But getting acceptance in the face of Shimano's component hegemony would not be easy. In fact SRAM had to sue Shimano in 1990 because the Masters of the Universe offered a 10 percent discount to bike makers who used an all-Shimano drivetrain when building bikes. That was too much money for a factory to leave on the table in such a competitive, close-margin business. Effectively, Grip Shift was frozen out of the most important part of the business, OEM orders.

Shimano settled the suit out of court so we don't know how much SRAM got, but we do know that from then on SRAM and other makers could compete and get OEM business from bike builders making Shimano-equipped bikes.

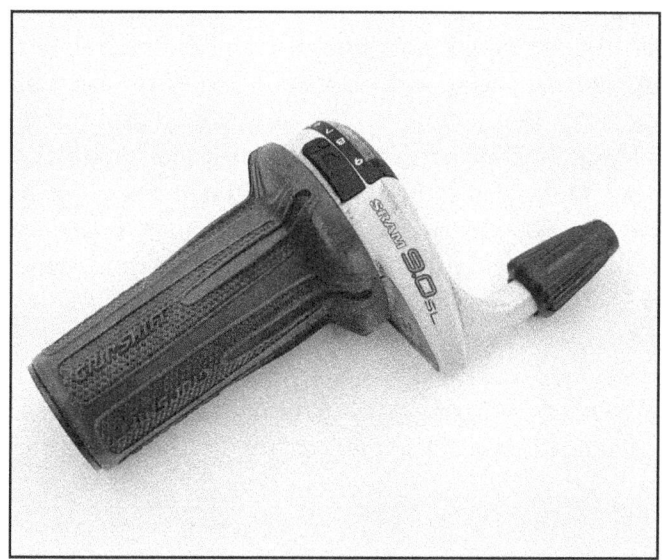

The 9-speed SRAM-Grip Shift

In 1991 SRAM brought out twist grip shifters for mountain bikes. But, the ambitious company was just getting started.

In 1995 they began producing its own derailleur, called ESP. In an even bigger move, in 1997 SRAM purchased the venerable European component maker Sachs. At one fell swoop this gave SRAM a complete component group, as Sachs had been on a buying spree purchasing several highly regarded European component makers.

From there SRAM continued to purchase other parts makers including suspension fork maker RockShox, which had defaulted on a loan from SRAM. Shortly thereafter SRAM moved the fork maker's production from Colorado Springs to Taiwan. SRAM also bought carbon-wheel maker

McGann

Zipp, Avid (maker of brakes, bars and stems), crankset maker Truvativ, and power-meter crank maker QUARQ. To top things off, in 2021 SRAM acquired pedal maker Time Sport from the Rossignol Group.

You name the bike component, SRAM could make it.

The result? SRAM believes that in 2023 it had a 15 percent share of the $3.5 billion bicycle component market with sales in 2020 of $974 million. Only clear-eyed, brilliant leadership could have transformed a firm making a set of gear shifters into a nearly one billion dollar behemoth.

Bikemag.com attributed some of SRAM's mountain bike success to their persistent pursuit of mountain bike national and world champion Greg Herbold. When they began talking with Herbold he was in the process of testing Shimano products. Though Herbold found the twist-grip shifters imperfect, he liked them and the company's owners, and began racing with SRAM equipment. Not long after, mountain bike cross country world champion and Pan-Am games gold medalist Tinker Juarez joined the Cannondale team and was racing with Grip Shift. The firm was on its way.

Tom French and founding Trek partner Bevil Hogg left Trek to start the Kestrel bike company, a pioneer in carbon fiber frames and components. The firm claimed that the 1986 Kestrel 4000 was the first all carbon-fiber production bicycle frame. Not long after, the company ran into trouble and was sold to Schwinn. Then Schwinn sold the brand and over time it had five or six owners. Its last owner was Advanced Sports, which was purchased by the Tiger Group in 2019, a liquidator specializing in troubled assets. As of this writing in early 2024 the brand seems to have been discontinued. There were plenty of other carbon-fiber frame makers in Asia to fill the void.

9
Heading into the 1990s

Asian bike makers had no intention of letting the Western manufacturers catch their breath.

Through the late 1980s Peugeot offered its top bike (compellingly named the PFC10Z) with a carbon frame equipped with a complete French component ensemble. By 1989 that included indexed Simplex (now owned by Ofmega) derailleurs, CLB side-pull brakes and a Solida aluminum cotterless crankset. Less expensive models used steel frames and Sachs-Huret indexed changers. All perfectly good product.

Looking for a way around the high import duties that Canada applied to bikes but not components, Canadian bike maker ProCycle began producing Peugeot bikes in Canada sometime in the 1970s. Even with importing separate components and frames and assembling the bike, there was a net savings. In 1987 ProCycle purchased the rights to market and sell those Peugeot bikes themselves in North America, an arrangement that lasted until 2001 when Swedish bike maker CycleEurope took over worldwide bicycle rights to the Peugeot bicycle brand.

Legendary French component maker Stronglight had invested heavily in state-of-the-art production machinery and despite the Asian onslaught, still had 300 employees in 1991. But by 2001, there were just 55 people on the Stronglight payroll. Component makers generally depend heavily on OEM business. With fewer surviving European factories available to place orders, the component makers had no choice but to let workers go.

Still, French inventiveness wasn't entirely stifled. Perhaps the only innovation to rival the importance of indexed shifting came from French ski binding maker Look. With rare exception, serious cyclists used to fix their feet to their pedals with toe clips and leather straps, using a slotted cleat that was nailed to the bottom of the shoe to hold the foot in place.

Jean Beyl was both a brilliant inventor and businessman. His work to protect athletes' joints goes back to 1950. Beyl broke his leg skiing while using the era's rigid ski bindings. That prompted him to revolutionize ski bindings with his Look Nevada binding, which allowed a skier's boot to release from the ski when the ski was severely twisted. He surely saved countless knees and ankles over the decades.

Given that what he invented was basically a twist-out ski binding, it's not surprising that it was Beyl who converted the ski-binding technology into the Look clipless pedal. In 1984 Look introduced (and patented) its *pédales automatiques*. They needed neither clips nor straps. A plastic cleat bolted to the bottom of the shoe snapped into a spring-loaded pedal. The rider could pull up and down on the pedal, then with just a horizontal twist of his foot, snap out. Brilliant. Bernard Hinault won the 1985 Tour de France using Look pedals and soon every serious cyclist had to have them.

Beyl sold the Look pedal and ski binding maker to businessman Bernard Tapie in 1983.

Initially, shoes of the era had to be drilled by the shop or the shoes' owners so that the new Look cleats could be bolted to the soles of the shoes. But very quickly shoe makers were offering shoes with holes drilled and tapped for both slotted cleats (suitable for toe clips and straps) and Look cleats. Shoes had so far not been designed to withstand the upward pull of the pedal stroke, toes straps had served that purpose. Shoe makers were soon offering product with more robust uppers that wouldn't give as the rider pulled up on his shoes.

There was a small problem. Traditional slotted cleats let the rider's foot rotate a bit as he turns the cranks. The movement is called "float". For most riders this is an essential part of the natural pedal stroke. The Look pedal initially held the foot rigidly in place and soon there were riders with knee and hip injuries. So, in 1987, another French company, Time Sport, introduced a clipless pedal with float. This firm had been started by Roland Cattin and his brilliant inventor father-in-law Jean Beyl.

Look didn't just let Time take over the performance pedal business. Look solved its problem by coming out with an optional red cleat that allowed the foot to rotate slightly.

This was not actually a brand-new idea: way back in 1895 American Charles Hanson received a patent for the clipless bicycle pedal. The rider would twist his foot to lock and unlock his foot from the deal. And, the pedal allowed the foot to rotate slightly through the crank's rotation. It had float! There were other clipless pedals, including our friend Cinelli's M-71, which required the rider to pull or push a locking rod to hold the pedal cleat in place. But it wasn't until Look's brilliant design came along that riders abandoned clips and straps.

Why Your Bike Is Made in Asia

Shimano's initial response to the clipless revolution was to license the Look patent. Shimano's resulting Dura-Ace 7401 pedal was a masterpiece of elegant, simple design. It was lighter and simpler than the Look equivalent and even allowed the rider to lean his bike further as he pedaled through a corner.

In the meantime, Shimano took the clipless concept and applied it to where the business really was, mountain bikes. In 1990 Shimano released its SPD (Shimano Pedaling Dynamics) mountain bike clipless pedal. It used a small cleat that fit into the recess of a mountain bike shoe sole, allowing the cleated rider to still run or walk. The pedal was double-sided, allowing a rider to cleat in without orienting the pedal. Shimano later inserted the tiny SPD mechanism into wider platform pedals, giving commuters the option of using clipless pedals with either cleated shoes or regular street shoes.

The Torelli Bormio clipless pedal, from Taiwan

Look's patent expired in 2004 and soon there was a flood of Look pedal copies coming out of Asia. Joining the other importers in 2006, I imported Torelli versions of both the Look road and Shimano SPD pedals, produced in a high-end Taiwan factory.

About the same time Look was taking over the pedal business, the company also began making superb carbon-fiber framesets that made the older lugged carbon frames from Vitus and Alan almost instantly obsolete.

Another European firm made a serious foray into the component marketplace. The ancient German bicycle component firm Fichtel & Sachs had been founded in the Bavarian town of Schweinfurt in 1895. The company's first products were ball bearings and bicycle hubs. German historians give Ernst Sachs credit for inventing a hub in 1898 that freewheeled. German historians also say he invented the coaster brake (back-pedal to stop) in 1903. American historians give others credit for these important inventions.

Fichtel & Sachs grew, becoming an important supplier to both the automotive and bicycle industries.

Looking to deepen its bicycle business, Fichtel & Sachs bought Huret in 1980. They didn't stop there. Through the decade, Fichtel & Sachs acquired several other well-known European parts makers, including French chain maker Sedis, hub and freewheel manufacturer Maillard, and Modolo, the Italian brake, bar and stem company. The eventual result was a complete component group, first called Sachs-Huret, and from 1987 just plain Sachs.

In the mid-1980s the American firm Todrys was running the U.S. distribution of Sachs-Huret. I liked the parts and felt they fitted nicely into our product line. After tossing the Vicini complete-bike project, we decided to assemble Torelli bikes in our warehouse.

In late 1988 our new Corsa Strada was an Italian frameset made by Ottavio Vicini's brother (SAB–Mario Vicini bicycles) assembled in our warehouse with a budget Sachs indexing group. That gave us an iron-clad control over the quality of our bikes. Each frame was tapped, faced and aligned in our warehouse and we built the wheels ourselves. The bikes went out and did not come back. We kept that business model as long as we owned Torelli, making all of our frames available with any group we carried. Our component selection grew to include Campagnolo, Shimano, Zeus, Gipiemme and Sachs.

During the late 1980s we received visits from a very nice gentleman whom I knew only as Mr. Hontani. I believe he was one of the founding executives of Shimano USA, but at this time he was representing Japanese companies. In 1987 he showed us a spectacular road frame branded Zunow, built by a Mr. Kageyama in Osaka. I was smitten and placed a small order. Their wonderfully fine workmanship was matched by their ride quality. The frame was made with specially drawn tubing with the seat tube flaring near the bottom bracket shell for greater stiffness. Every aspect of the bike shouted care, precision and thoughtfulness.

We carried Zunow framesets and some Zunow bottom bracket shells and tubing until the end of 1989. Like so many bike makers, Zunow wanted a distributor who would sell more frames. They yanked the distributorship from us to find a better marketer. I don't think they found another USA distributor. Over and over again I heard small builders and component makers say some version of "America is a very large country", and expect extraordinary sales numbers that no one ever meets. I would show them the number of performance riders in the country to explain why sales per

Why Your Bike Is Made in Asia

capita were lower in the US than in European countries and their eyes would glaze over. They simply did not want to have their minds confused with facts.

We were interested in bringing in a mountain bike. Hontani set us up with Yokota, at that time a contract builder, that is, a firm that made bikes for other companies. They produced our Dirt Research mountain bike. We did a couple of containers of them, but there were two problems. First, it was another brand to market when we had our hands full with Mondonico, Torelli, Faggin, Masi and Zunow.

Second, we really had no business selling mountain bikes. Even though the bike was a good value and well-spec'd and had the usual superb Japanese workmanship, we had trouble selling them because it was a new brand being sold by a firm that otherwise had no presence in the mountain bike market. After a couple of short container loads we abandoned a project we never should have started. Surprisingly, after we quit the mountain bike project, Yokota continued to market their own bikes under the Dirt Research name with a slightly modified version of our original graphics. We had never trademarked it, didn't know about it and it certainly didn't matter to us.

In the mid-1980s Sachs was selling re-branded Huret derailleurs with cosmetic changes. The parts line did not match the best Italian and European components' styling, but they were simple, well-made, nicely priced and worked well. My customers and I could live without pretty.

But in 1987, just two years after Shimano had dropped the SIS bomb, Sachs came out with its own indexing system, called Aris. This was an indexed system that worked, and worked well. In what turned out to be a mixed blessing for us, that same year Sachs was acquired by the giant Mannesmann group. Sachs wasn't a walking-wounded company like SunTour or a firm that had contempt for what its customers desired like Campagnolo. Every year saw improvements in the Sachs product line.

In about 1989 Sachs slightly re-styled its parts line, making them look smooth and up-to-date. The firm also began collaborating with Campagnolo. The result was several of the Sachs high end parts that had been produced by Mannesmann-owned firms such as crankset maker Thun were now supplied by the Italian firm. In 1991 the Sachs New Success Crankset was a re-branded Campagnolo Athena crankset.

Sachs' ambition became even clearer when the firm opened an American warehouse and sales office run by industry veteran John Neugent, former product manager at distributor Service Cycle.

McGann

Sachs' collaboration with Campagnolo grew ever deeper. In 1993 Sachs-branded Campagnolo Ergopower integrated brake-shift levers were released, a year after the Campagnolo-branded levers were first sold. False rumors still abound that Sachs had designed the complex machinery of the Ergopower lever for Campagnolo and Sachs' right to sell the levers under their own name was part of the deal.

Sachs was also making quality mountain bike parts that more than one writer said competed with Shimano's renowned XTR at a much lower price.

As the Sachs product line evolved, a greater emphasis was placed on mountain bike and touring components.

Yet, for all the success Sachs was having, the gigantic Mannesmann firm found it to be more bother than it was worth.

Sachs USA boss John Neugent tried to put together a group of bike industry executives to buy Sachs, but the changed emphasis from road racing components to mountain bikes and road touring made the product line attractive to American component maker SRAM. As we've seen, when the smoke had cleared in 1997, SRAM owned Sachs, one of the oldest firms in the cycle industry. At the time Sachs was a $125 million a year company with 1,250 employees. In 1999 SRAM ceased using the Sachs name.

That put an end to Torelli's Sachs distribution. Going into 1998 we carried just two groups: Campagnolo in depth, including small parts for shop repairs, and Shimano, as what is called an OEM (original equipment manufacturer) account, only for building complete bikes.

Meanwhile, at about the same time, Faggin's French distributor Alvarez was selling Faggins directly to retail customers in the US. We protested the, well, grey-marketing, which the reader might recall we had done for a short time with Mavic. But since Alvarez was a huge distributor of Faggin, the family took no action. Seeing no other way out, we closed out our stock of Faggins while we were dumping our Mavic inventory after Mavic had gone dealer-direct.

10
The industry moves to Asia

In the 1980s, Huffy had been on a tear. It had closed all but one of its manufacturing plants, having nearly all of its bikes made in Celina, Ohio. The firm was making an astounding two million bicycles a year. But the company was selling them to just a few huge retailers, a result of the 1980s mass-market retail consolidation. And Huffy was selling at least half its bikes to the largest retailer in the world, Walmart.

Walmart plays hardball. The company had justly earned its nickname "The Bully of Bentonville". When Walmart gave Huffy a 900,000 bike order in the mid-1990s, it was doing the bike maker no favors. Walmart demanded a lower price for its bikes. Much lower. So low, in fact, that Huffy went to its unionized work force and asked for a pay cut so that it could sell the bikes above cost. Huffy was able to turn a profit for a couple of years.

But the relentless pricing pressure from Walmart never stopped. Even with the workers taking a pay cut and the firm doing all it could to lower its manufacturing costs, Huffy had to close its giant Celina, Ohio plant.

On September 28, 1999, the Associated Press had a short news item that told a story about not only the bicycle business, but about American manufacturing in general. The Huffy Corporation announced that by the end of the year it would stop making bicycles in the United States and would close its two non-union manufacturing plants located in Farmington, Missouri, and Southhaven, Mississippi. It would have all of it bikes made "with partners around the world". The company said this would finish the firm's transformation from a single-brand manufacturer to a multi-brand design, marketing and distribution company.

Still, with Chinese workers making less than a half-dollar an hour producing its bikes, Huffy could not sell its bikes profitably.

Amid accounting irregularities and accusations of company misuse of its pension funds, Huffy declared bankruptcy in October of 2004. Huffy's assets were taken over by its Chinese creditors. Despite having an office in the U.S., the 100-year old company was no longer an American firm.

As some bicycle firms thrived and others struggled, the biggest component company in the world was Shimano. No one else was even close. Frank Berto estimated that in 1995 Shimano had an 85 percent share of the market for quality parts for multi-speed bikes. Berto further noted that Shimano had fifteen component groups: five road, four mountain and six comfort bike. By 2008 the company had expanded its range to twenty-three groups, all of it well-designed and competitively priced. It seemed that every day Shimano had a new product or an incremental improvement in some aspect of a component. The other parts makers had an opponent that did not sleep.

Shimano at this point had only one real challenger, SRAM.

The bicycle business was now Asian, though with subtle shift. Japan became an expensive place to make commodities, so at first the makers went to Taiwan. But relentless competition drove the majority of production to mainland China with Taiwan becoming the mid-to high end product maker. By the mid-2000s, China was making more than two-thirds of Planet Earth's bicycles.

What a change. In 1968 Schwinn had produced more than one million bicycles and in 1973 the top six American bike factories made about nine million bikes. In 2008, American bike production was barely a statistical blip on the production radar, an estimated 200,000 bikes.

And Schwinn, which had opened that factory in Greenville, Mississippi? Schwinn finally shuttered it in 1991 after suffering losses estimated at $30 million. Schwinn had done all it could to make a go of the plant, even pricing its foreign production higher to protect sales of Greenville-made product. Ed Schwinn had even sent his brother Richard to try to make the factory profitable. Richard had an MBA and had worked on the floor of the Chicago factory. But it wasn't to be. Schwinn no longer had the know-how to run a bike factory.

At this point in Schwinn's long history, the firm was losing money on bicycles, but making such big money on the AirDynes that the firm's fundamental problems were masked. That was fine with Ed Schwinn, who did not want to hear any bad news from the company's financial arm.

Then things got worse. Sears began selling a version of the AirDyne for hundreds of dollars less. Schwinn tried taking Sears to court for infringing on what Schwinn asserted was a proprietary design. The judge wasn't having any of that and Sears was allowed to keep on wrecking the sales of the product Schwinn was depending upon for survival.

Why Your Bike Is Made in Asia

By 1990 the days of profitability were again ending. The firm lost close to $3 million that year and had a debt of $80 million. Schwinn's bankers were worried. Yet, at a meeting with his bankers at Schwinn headquarters, Ed treated the men and women he depended upon for survival badly.

In 1991 the first banker pulled the trigger, sending its Schwinn loan to a corporate collection agency (these people have the gentle name of "workout specialists"). As Schwinn violated its loan covenants, the banks got tougher with the bike firm, working hard to reduce their exposure to the troubled bike maker.

Still, Ed Schwinn continued to treat the men who were keeping his company going with contempt, even blowing off meetings without notice. It was certainly a misplaced self-confidence. In 1991 the firm lost $23.3 million and in 1992 things continued to deteriorate as Ed talked to potential buyers, of course overvaluing the company and mismanaging every aspect of recapitalizing Schwinn.

On October 8, 1992, Schwinn filed for protection under Chapter 11 of the United States Bankruptcy Code. The company had gone from 28 percent of the US market in the 1960s to 8 percent at the time of the filing.

The filing caught the country's attention. In interviews Ed Schwinn took no responsibility for the company's troubles, blaming it instead on a troubled economy and his bankers' refusal to lend him the funds he wanted.

Ed Schwinn had visions of using the bankruptcy to turn the company around. That was not to be. The creditors and suppliers were owed far too much. Their plan was for an auction of the firm when a group of investors led by Sam Zell began maneuvering to purchase what was left of Schwinn.

To this bike mechanic it was a lengthy, complex transaction. The sale was finally consummated on January 19, 1993. Sam Zell's Zell-Chilmark fund bought the company. The Chicago offices were shuttered and the company was moved to Boulder, Colorado.

Zell-Chilmark disposed of the Schwinn's stake in the Hungarian factory by selling it to a Russian/Hungarian duo who continued to use the Schwinn name.

By 1995, under the new ownership Schwinn was again profitable and producing bikes people wanted, but without any Schwinn family members involved. Nor were any Schwinns produced in an American factory.

Innovation was hitting the high end as well. In 1984 steel bicycles underwent a real change. In the early 1980s Italian framebuilder Alberto Masi (son and heir of bike building legend Faliero Masi) started experimenting with thin-walled, oversized steel tubing joined with internal investment-cast

McGann

lugs. In 1984 he unveiled the result, the Masi Tre Volumetrica. The bike was stunning. Through the use of thin-wall tubing the bigger tubed-frame remained light. The internal lugs gave the thin tubes more support. And the ride? Simply outstanding. The bike had a solid feel, the fatter tubes giving the frames increased torsional rigidity, yet the steel fork with a flat fork crown (allowing for longer, more flexible blades) and seat stays brazed to the side of the seat lug made the bike quite comfortable to ride.

Eventually the oversize, thin-wall steel tube became the standard. Columbus began producing EL-OS tubing in 1991, made from their Nivacrom steel alloy. Traditional tubesets SL, SLX and TSX had 1-inch top tubes, 1⅛-inch seat and down tubes. Through the magic of higher-strength steel that allowed thinner walls, An EL-OS frame with 1⅛-inch top and seat tube and 1¼-inch down tube weighed about a half-pound less than its smaller-tubed cousins.

Antonio Mondonico started sending me EL-OS frames in the spring of 1992. They were a hit.

The Torelli Nitro Express, originally made from EL-OS tubing by Antonio Mondonico

To this writer, the ride quality was much finer and that impression seemed to be the consensus of riders, racers and writers everywhere. Quickly EL-OS and variations of its basic dimensions became the standard material for building frames for the professional road teams.

Columbus trickled its oversized steel tubing technology down its line. In 1994 Columbus produced oversized Thron Tubing, made from the same

Why Your Bike Is Made in Asia

Cyclex steel alloy that was used in making SL and SLX tubing. Soon all of Mondonico's frames were oversized as were all but two of Torelli's least expensive frames. By 1998 all steel frames I was selling, from the least expensive to the finest, were oversized.

But in 1998, it wasn't just steel frames that we were selling. Columbus had been making aluminum tubing and though it went against my steel-worship religion, we began selling frames from Columbus' Altec-II aluminum tubing, which we called the Alu-Wing, as well as a lugged carbon frame from one of the pioneers of carbon tubing, Alan of Italy.

In for a dime, in for a dollar. The next year we began importing a frame made in Italy to our specifications out of Oria's 7020 heat-treatable aluminum tubing. Aluminum 7020 was the perfect alloy for bicycles, in that after heat-treating, it age-hardened naturally after welding. We called that frame the Spada, Italian for Sword, and for years the Spada was our best-selling frame.

The Alu-Wing wholesaled for $800.00 and weighed just 2.8 pounds for a 56-centimeter frame while the better-selling Spada wholesaled for $560.00 and weighed in at 3.6 pounds. Both frames were made in northern Italy.

In 2000 we began a running change, having all of the Torelli steel frames, except the top-of-the-line Nitro Express, tig-welded, while the Mondonico frames remained lugged. That gave us both a better product differentiation between the two lines and it slightly lightened the Torelli frames. Our entry-level Corsa Strada frame, now made of Oria Vanadium tubing dropped below four pounds.

By 2000 Campagnolo was producing nice mid-range components in their Mirage and Veloce groups. Mid-range for us regular mortals, low-end for Campagnolo. And over at the Columbus factory there was a new tubing called Zona made from Nivacrom steel drawn down to just 0.5mm and one called New Thron, also drawn to 0.5mm. I was sure that if I found the right builder putting these two pieces together would yield terrific made-in-Italy bikes.

I was right. We found a superb northern Italian builder with a tiny shop and just five employees, including the owner and his secretary, to produce two different bikes. The Brianza was a higher-performance road machine made from tig-welded Zona tubing and equipped with a Veloce/Mirage mixed groupset. The Gran Sasso bike was named after the highest peak in the Apeninnes (and where Mussolini was imprisoned until he was freed by German commandos in 1943). It had a Campagnolo Mirage triple group mated to a Columbus New Thron tubing tig-welded frameset. The bikes were a hit. We were able to sell the Brianza with its original specifications until 2003. But the Gran Sasso with its triple crankset and available low gears was what our customers really wanted. We imported and sold that bike through 2005, when a combination of macroeconomic factors, including a collapsing dollar and a troubled Italian bike industry, forced us to discontinue the bike.

In 2001 I was again reminded why Italy was such a wonderful place to do business. I had been in close communication with the sales director of Columbus, Claudio Marra, discussing ways to improve the Torelli line. He made me an offer I could not refuse. He offered a tubeset with a Nivacrom main triangle drawn to 0.7-0.4-0.7mm with Cyclex (basically old Columbus SL) fork blades and rear triangle for an incredible price. The front triangle was essentially the same tubes Columbus was using for its Nemo tubeset. I jumped at it. After consulting with Signor Marra we called it Torelli/Nemo747 and used it for several Torelli framesets as well as the Mondonico Futura Leggero. It was a hit, and we sold countless 747 frames, some all steel, some with carbon forks, some with wishbone carbon seat stays.

We had become serious importers in 1981, the year we date the beginning of Torelli, which meant that 2001 was our twentieth anniversary. To celebrate our having come this far we offered 100 special Twentieth Anniversary framesets. They were built by Antonio and Mauro Mondonico and had special red/white/green Italian flag paint jobs, anniversary-engraved bottom bracket shell and fork crown, special graphics and new external investment-cast dropouts. Each was numbered, 1/100, etc. I almost wept with joy when the 100 framesets quickly sold out.

The next year it became clear that the traditional-diameter tubed and lugged Super Strada was obsolete and had few buyers, forcing us to discontinue what was to me an old friend.

In 2002 we had a surprising success. I had wanted to sell a modern titanium frame, but had not figured out how to do it and be competitive. I got a call from the east coast one day from a fellow claiming to represent a Russian firm building titanium bicycle frames. With the cold war now over, we were told that there were skilled titanium fabricators in Russia who used to work in the arms industry and were now making bicycle frames and they were looking for customers. We ordered a sample. Expecting a poorly-made frame built to what we had always heard were low standards of Russian manufacture, we were stunned by the excellence of the workmanship. And when we built it into a bike it handled with classic Italian perfection. The company making the frames had done its homework. We were hooked and

Why Your Bike Is Made in Asia

began importing and selling them as Torelli Titanio frames. Indicative of their extraordinary quality, we had no returns, no frame failures and sold them for years.

We were now selling frames out of steel, aluminum and titanium and offering to build them up in both Shimano (105, Ultegra and Dura-Ace) and all of the Campagnolo groups. Plus we were importing Brianza and Gran Sasso complete Italian-made bikes.

Change was coming. We wanted to have a top-quality carbon fork. At this point that meant Taiwan sourcing. Our good friend John Neugent pointed us in the right direction, telling us who to use as a trading agent because one didn't buy directly from the factory, which was news to me.

We ended up with a trading company that had a man who was mad about bicycles who jumped at the chance to handle our account and facilitate our purchases for higher end product. He told us to call him "James", which was his "nom de l'entreprise", explaining that we would not be able to say his real name.

James knew who made good product in Taiwan and arranged for us to get sample forks, one all carbon with a carbon steering tube and one with carbon blades with an aluminum fork crown and steering tube. Wary in our first Asian transaction, we sent the forks to a destruction lab to test them. We got the report back that they finally shut off their machine that was flexing and releasing the forks over and over and over again, hour after hour, day after day. They could not break the forks. So we placed our order and indeed, the forks were simply superb and held up in the field as well as they did in the destruction lab. We were now importers of Asian goods. We sold those carbon forks as Torelli brand forks in both versions.

The cycling world was quickly embracing non-ferrous frames and we tried hard to supply what the riders were demanding. We continued with our Spada aluminum frame and added a model we called Stiletto, which was built from a then-advanced aluminum alloy from Columbus, called Altec II. Altec II was made from 7005 aluminum alloy which has the terrific advantage of not needing heat treating after welding, reducing the trouble and cost of using the alloy. Plus, we added a carbon fiber rear triangle, supplied by Columbus.

And that carbon fiber rear triangle, branded Carve by Columbus, was not made in Italy, as I had supposed when I designed the bike. As one might expect, it was made in Asia where the ability to produce reliable, well-made state-of-the-art carbon bicycle components was at its most advanced. Once again, the western world had let a budding technology that would become an essential part of cycle manufacturing slip through its fingers.

McGann

We also offered Reynolds carbon forks, which were made in the United States. Not everything high-tech went east.

Business can be complicated. An importer not only has to take into account the price his supplier charges, but since that will in some way or another be priced in his native currency, exchange-rates matter a lot. Our Taiwan suppliers quoted in US dollars, but of course they would have to convert the US dollars to New Taiwan dollars to use them in Taiwan. European continental suppliers quoted in Euros. And to show how our life had changed, in 2000 the Euro fell to $0.89. The products of Europe were on sale and it made selling them both easy and profitable for us. But it was difficult for American manufacturers who could not compete in foreign markets when the price of their products were converted to their foreign customers' currency.

That began to change on late 2002 as the Dollar began to fall in value.

By the end of 2004 the Euro had risen to $1.35, and it kept on climbing, reaching an historic peak in mid-2008 of $1.58.

Now the shoe was on the other foot. At first, we absorbed the increased costs, but we could only do that for a short while. We, like all other importers, had to surrender and raise our prices.

2005 brought about a new world for us. The first, and not unexpected news was that with the dollar's devaluation and declining demand for steel frames, the Mondonicos told us that they would stop building frames at the end of 2005. Plus, Antonio had worked like a dog his whole life and was deservedly ready to retire.

Given the increasing popularity of cyclo-cross, we thought it would be a good idea to add Guerciotti, who made cross his specialty, to our line. In other times it would have been a home run, but with the very strong Euro, it was a tough sell.

The year also saw the first Asian-made Torelli frame. It was time. The Toccata was made with carbon tubes joined with internal aluminum lugs. It was a hit.

Mauro and Antonio had been coming over each fall to travel with me all over the U.S. to measure customers for custom-made frames. The Mondonicos kindly agreed to come one more time to visit shops all over the country and go home with a full order book.

While we were in Norwalk Connecticut to visit one of our very best customers, Alex Stanek, owner of Smart Cycles, my life changed. In the motel the evening after visiting the shop and measuring a long line of customers, I felt a terrible pain in my left eye. It got worse and finally, in absolute misery I made my way to the Mondonicos' room and banged on

Why Your Bike Is Made in Asia

their door. I told them that I was very ill and had to go to the hospital. They quickly dressed and drove our rental car with me in the back seat to the hospital.

That evening the doctors could not figure out what was wrong with me but by morning I had developed a painful rash around my one good eye (I had put a wire in my right eye when I was seven). They told me that I had shingles, an infection of a nerve and the skin around it. Shingles is caused by the same virus that causes chickenpox. Once you get chickenpox, the virus never leaves your body and can remain dormant the rest of your life. If the body's immunity is lowered, the chickenpox virus can become active again, manifesting itself as this painful rash. At that time there was no vaccine for shingles.

I had never felt this bad in my life. Ever.

I called my wife Carol and explained where things stood. She bought me a plane ticket home. The Mondonicos drove me to the airport and saw me off. Good guys that they were, they continued the measuring Tour by themselves and flew all over the country measuring customers and taking orders for frames and bikes.

I managed to get on board the plane and find my seat. I was expecting to be told I couldn't fly since I looked like I had some terrible disease (which I did). My face was terribly disfigured and I could barely walk. But I sat down and kept still and no one bothered me.

When I staggered off the plane in Santa Barbara, Carol was there waiting for me to take me home. She had already set up an appointment with our ophthalmologist. He gave me a careful examination, prescribed painkillers and sent me home. There was really nothing that could be done except let the disease run its course.

It took a while. After the rash had cleared up and I could do some work I started coming to the office. But I tired easily and had to take naps a few times a day.

Finding that I just didn't have the fortitude to do my share of running Torelli we tried hiring a professional manager. After a short while it became clear we weren't a good match and we parted ways. Carol and I went back to running the show ourselves.

We were fortunate that the man managing our warehouse, Steve Anderson, took on the burden of making up for my absence and inability to do my job properly. He ran Torelli when we were gone and uncomplainingly accepted the increased work load. I will always be grateful for his kindness, intelligence and incredible work ethic.

Back to the business of importing.

McGann

We continued to move product sourcing from Europe to Asia. By the end of 2006 almost our entire parts catalogue was Asian-made, though we still brought in a few Italian steel frames.

Some of the product supplier changes were generated by the turmoil the currency fluctuations caused. Some by simply ambitious manufacturers understandably trying to increase sales.

Paolo Guerciotti turned the management of his business over to his son, who found our representation inadequate. He told us we would no longer be his American importer and that he would find another distributor, which he did.

For years we had been distributing Vittoria shoes. The beautifully hand-made shoes were made in Northern Italy. But, we were not able to move them in the numbers we had in the past because of the dollar's fall. Vittoria told us that they had to pull the agency from us, which, again, we understood. I never learned my lesson that when you distribute another company's product, it is their product, not your own.

We kept on adding new Torelli-brand products, almost all of them sourced in Taiwan, including carbon fiber rims and wheels built with them, saddles, carbon and aluminum seat posts, stems, pedals and cleats.

We had been importing Italian-made Sapo pumps for years, but that old Italian firm became a casualty of the currency fluctuations as well as relentless pressure from well-made Asian competition. We were able to quickly source Taiwan-made pumps that were superbly made. As I type this, a fourteen-year-old Taiwan-made Torelli Amalfi floor pump sits in my garage and still reliably pumps up both my bike's tires and my car tires. It has a brilliant pump head that works on both Presta and Schrader valves.

Things were humming along nicely with a completely renewed catalogue of up-to-date, very competitively price product, making sales a much easier job.

There was just one problem. Me. I still found doing the hard work of working at Torelli simply beyond me. Plus, my parents who lived halfway across the country were in failing health and required regular trips to Arkansas to care for them.

So in September 2007 we sold Torelli Imports, keeping the portion of the website that reported race results so that we could promote the cycling books we published. We still update it almost every day, www.bikeraceinfo.com.

It was the end of a chapter of our lives that when I look back on it, I can't believe how lucky we were. We had a job that took us all over the world

Why Your Bike Is Made in Asia

and let us meet so many people that we still call friends, and gave us a good living for decades doing something we loved.

As Carol and I moved on to a new life, the bicycle industry's ferocious competition continued unabated. When we sold Torelli there were the three major players in the component business, Shimano, SRAM and Campagnolo. Plus there were smaller firms in Taiwan including SR SunTour, SunRace, Long Yih (which I had never heard of until I began researching this book) and Falcon.

Shimano was the big dog and still is as I write this in early 2024. The firm remains the largest bicycle component manufacturer in the world. It was estimated that at the end of 2022 the firm had a 50 percent market share for all bicycle components and a 70 percent share of the high-end range. Touting the value of its stock, one financial web site called it a "bike component monopoly at an attractive price". Successfully competing with the relentless component maker was not a job for the faint of heart.

The firm that stepped up to the plate and started hitting home runs was American component maker SRAM. By 2007 the firm had factories all over the world, including the U.S., Mexico, France, Taiwan and China. At the time the company had three well-regarded road groups.

By 2023 the majority of SRAM's parts were made in Taiwan and China.

Campagnolo kept making small improvements to its line, using carbon fiber to make ever lighter parts. In 2007 the firm produced a crankset design called Ultra-Torque with an interesting innovation. The bottom bracket had a hollow spindle that was split in the middle. The two center ends of the spindle had tapered teeth that meshed together. This design, called a "Hirth joint" allowed a lighter spindle and wider spacing of the bottom bracket bearings. Campagnolo called it Ultra-Torque and still uses that design.

But, with its manufacturing plant in Italy, that valuable OEM business that Asian component makers have is basically unavailable to Campagnolo. The firm remains innovative and an important niche player, but the days of Campagnolo getting lots of OEM spec are, for now, gone.

The largest manufacturer of bicycles in the world is Taiwan's Giant Manufacturing, which made 6.6 million bicycles in 2017 with revenue of $1.9 billion. That revenue grew to $2.93 billion in 2021.

Let's fast-forward to 2022 to see who was selling the bikes bought by the U.S. and the world. Writer Daniel Workman compiled these numbers for bicycle exports by country for 2022 (values are US dollars). These fifteen countries shipped 87.1 percent of bicycle exports in 2022. These numbers are a bit deceptive because the component groups on most of the non-Asian bikes are, in fact, Asian.

1. China: $3.8 billion (30.5% of exported bicycles)
2. Taiwan: $1.6 billion (13.3%)
3. Germany: $935.5 million (7.6%)
4. Cambodia: $899.8 million (7.2%)
5. Netherlands: $843.3 million (6.8%)
6. Italy: $368.8 million (3%)
7. Portugal: $362.2 million (2.9%)
8. Spain: $336.6 million (2.7%)
9. Vietnam: $327.5 million (2.7%)
10. Belgium: $312.2 million (2.5%)
11. Bulgaria: $204.6 million (1.7%)
12. Indonesia: $203.1 million (1.6%)
13. Bangladesh: $192.5 million (1.6%)
14. Poland: $186.8 million (1.5%)
15. United States: $171.2 million (1.4%)

Of these countries, Asian exports totaled 56.6%, European exports (with largely Asian componentry) were 27% of the sales listed. American sales were 1.4%.

Writer Jeff Ferry wrote that China makes over 60% of the world's bikes. I assume this includes domestic consumption. He cited these numbers for the U.S. bike market:

Domestic production: 300,000 (2.2% of market)
China: 10.2 million (76.5%). Some statisticians put the China's U.S. market share as high as 86%.
Cambodia: 1.3 million (10.1%)
Taiwan: 856,150 (6.4%)
Vietnam: 270,539 (2.0 %)

In other words, Americans ride Asian bikes.

A former factory manager explained the insidious process that either shrank or shuttered many European bicycle factories. "I need some hubs and none can be had locally. An agent says he can get them for me quickly in Asia, and for a lower price. The transaction goes according to plan and

Why Your Bike Is Made in Asia

I have hubs to keep my production going. Next time, rather than getting the European hubs, I go back to the Taiwan factory for more hubs and have pedals added to the order. There's room in the container and it's no particular trouble for anyone.

"Then rims. After a couple of orders of hubs and rims, I'm asked if I would like to have the wheels built in Taiwan. Now I have no need of my wheel-building machinery or workers. Each container gets a few more parts and then I add some frames. The frames are good, cheap and delivered on time. I paint and decal them in the factory and add them to my production. It's a short step to having the frames painted and decaled in Taiwan. And then, why assemble them in Italy? Why not have the bikes assembled and boxed in Asia?"

Thus, step by step, less of the bike's content is European and more and more is Asian until finally the factory is a warehouse. This process was replicated all over Italy with the same devastating result. An industry that had supported skilled artisans for generations vanished in a few short years. No one thought he was going to shut down his production. It just came out that way.

Claudio Marra, who has spent a lifetime working with and managing both Italian and Asian bicycle companies, says the reasons for the migration are complex. He described a market where customers were not only being pulled to Asia by low costs, they were being pushed there by Italian producers. He remembered working for one high-end frame builder who had a capacity to produce about 7,000 frames a year, but some years was receiving orders for 100,000 frames. "They refused to invest in their factories," he lamented, preferring to bank their profits rather than expand their production. Compare this attitude to the Japanese and Taiwanese industrialists who were willing to gamble and take on gut-wrenching levels of debt to improve their factories. Yet, the importers and distributors still needed product and if one builder or one country would not sell them what they needed, they could and would go elsewhere.

Marra contrasted the complacent European culture where a customer's purchase order could be blithely turned down with the usual Taiwanese response. "If a customer comes to a busy Taiwan factory with a large order, he'll most likely be told that the order cannot be fulfilled immediately, but some production time could be found to make some product now and the rest of the order would somehow be worked into the year's production schedule." A customer would not be allowed to walk away if it was at all possible.

McGann

And what about those Europeans who did survive? Why were they still in business when so many of their compatriots were shuttering their factories? Walter Calesso, manager of high-end component producer Fac Michelin said that no small measure of audacity was needed. "We are in business because my boss is crazy." When faced with declining orders for their existing mid-range products, the factory took a chance and invested huge sums in designing and manufacturing high-end, value-added components. Further, Fac Michelin, whose product line is marketed under the brand Miche, also spent a fortune in marketing, going so far as to sponsor their own professional cycling team. Calesso said his boss was acutely conscious that shuttering his factory would destroy the lives of the workers who had made a career of working at Miche. Saving the factory whose business was an important part of the area's economy was a responsibility management took seriously.

But Miche's story is a rare one.

Tomorrow morning I'll go do my errands around town riding my Mongoose commuter bike made in Taiwan.

Bibliography

Berto, Frank. *The Dancing Chain, History and Development of the Derailleur Bicycle*. Third edition. San Francisco, California: Cycle Publishing/Van der Plas Publications, 2009.

Crown, Judith & Glenn Coleman. *No Hands: The Rise and Fall of the Schwinn Bicycle Company, an American Institution*. New York, New York: Henry Holt and Company, 1996.

Guroff, Margaret. *The Mechanical Horse, How the Bicycle Reshaped American Life*. Austin, Texas: University of Texas Press, 2016.

Halberstam, David. *The Reckoning*. London, UK: Bloomsbury Publishing, 1987.

Hayduk, Douglas. *Bicycle Merallurgy for the Cyclist*. Boulder, Colorado: Johnson Publishing Company, 1987.

Herlihy, David. *Bicycle: The History*. New Haven, Connecticut: Yale University Press, 2004.

Moore, Richard. *Slaying the Badger: Greg LeMond, Bernard Hinault and the Greatest Tour de France*. Boulder Colorado: Velo Press, 2012.

Nye, Peter Joffre. *The Fast Times of Albert Champion, From Record-setting Racer to Dashing Tycoon, an Untold Story of Speed, Success, and Betrayal*. Amherst, New York: Prometheus Books, 2014.

Nye, Peter Joffre. *Hearts of Lions, The History of American Bicycle Racing*. Lincoln, Nebraska: University of Nebraska Press, 2020.

Parkinson, C. Northcote. *East and West*. Boston, Massachusetts: Houghton Mifflin Company, 1963.

Pridmore, Jay & Jim Hurd. *Schwinn Bicycles*. Osceola, Wisconsin: Motorbooks International, 1996.

Pridmore, Jay & Jim Hurd. *The American Bicycle*. Osceola, Wisconsin: Motorbooks International, 1995.

Rosen, Jody. *Two Wheels Good: The History and Mystery of the Bicycle*. New York, New York: Crown, 2022.

Smith, Robert. *A Social History of the Bicycle, Its Early Life and Times in America*. New York, New York: American Heritage Press, 1972.

Sutherland, Howard. *Sutherland's Handbook for Bicycle Mechanics*. Fourth edition. Berkeley, California: Sutherland Publications, 1985.

Witherell, James. *Bicycle History: A Chronological Cycling History of People, Races, and Technology*, 2nd ed. McMinnville, Oregon: McGann Publishing, 2016.

Woodland, Les. *Dirty Feet: How the great unwashed created the Tour de France*. McMinnville, Oregon: McGann Publishing, 2021.

Woodland, Les. *The Yellow Jersey Companion to the Tour de France*. London, UK: Yellow Jersey Press, 2007.

Websites: Here are a few of the many consulted over the years.
    bikeraceinfo.com
    cyclingnews.com
    gallica.bnf.fr
    wikipedia.org

Conversations, letters and emails over the years with so many people, among them: the late Owen Mulholland, Les Woodland, Steve Lubanski, Cino Cinelli, Celestino Vercelli, Greg LeMond, Paolo Guerciotti, Antonio and Mauro Mondonico, Faliero Masi, the late Howie Cohen, John Neugent, Larry Theobald, David L. Stanley and Pat Brady.

Index

A

Adidas 7, 104
ADR cycling team 103
Advanced Sports 124
AirDyne 132
Alan 127, 135
Allez 110
Allvit 27, 31, 33, 64, 69
Alpina 101
Altec II 135, 137
Alu-Wing 135
Alvarez 106, 130
Ambrosio 102, 107
American Commercial Bank 72
American Eagle Olympic 60
AMF 46, 48
Anderson, Steve 139
Anquetil, Jacques 14
Anthony, Susan B. 19
Apeninnes 135
Arab-Israeli war 50
Aris 129
Arnold, Adolf Frederick William 36
Arnold, Schwinn & Company 35, 39
Ashtabula forks 86
Asia 9, 49, 67, 74, 83, 101, 102,
    106-107, 111, 116, 124-125, 127, 131-
    132, 137, 138, 140-143
ASO 105
Atala 29
Atax 31
Athena 129
Atlas Cycle 53
Atom freewheels 76
Autolined 106
Avid 124

B

Baldini, Ercole 80
Bangladesh 142
Baudry de Saunier, Louis 14
Belgium 26, 142
Berto, Frank 5, 27, 34, 116, 132, 145
Beyl, Jean 125-126
Bianchi 29
Bicycling Magazine 77
Bike Ribbon 107
Bill's Bike Shop 7, 74-75, 81
BMX 73, 85-88, 107-108, 110-111,
    113, 118-120
Bobet, Louison 28
Boneshakers 18
Bourrelier group 104
Boy's Life 43
Bozzi, Emilio 80
Brandt, Jobst 110
Breeze, Joe 110
Brianza 135-137
Bridgestone 51, 68
Brooks 34
Bruno 102, 103
BSA 34
Bulgaria 142
Burch, Ray 42-43
Burke, Richard 122

C

Calesso, Walter 144
Camarillo Bicycle Center 7-8, 76-79
Cambodia 142
Campagnolo 26-28, 30-33, 64-65,
    69-70, 73, 79-81, 97, 100, 103, 107, 110,
    117-118, 128-130, 135, 137, 141

147

Campagnolo, Tullio................ 26, 117
Canada 50, 125
Cannondale 93, 124
Captain Kangaroo.................... 43
Carbon-fiber....................22, 124, 127
Carlisle 54
Carlton 34
Carve 137
Cattin, Roland...................... 126
Célérifère 14
Centurion 9-10, 46-47, 67-68, 80-82
Chain Bike Corp.................... 46
Chevrolet Bel Air................... 57
Chicago 35, 39, 41, 43, 47, 51, 108, 118, 120-122, 132-133
China................ 106, 122, 132, 141, 142
China Bicycles...................... 122
Chopper............................. 45
Chrysler 32
Cinelli............89-90, 98, 100, 105, 108, 126, 146
C. Itoh 68
Citroën 29
Clarks Cables................... 105-106, 114
CLB................................ 31, 125
Clipless pedal 126, 127
Cohen, Howie 5, 53-63, 67, 87, 88, 146
Cohen, RosaBelle............ 56-57, 59, 63
Cohen Sr., Leo 53-56
Coleman, Glenn........ 5, 39, 42-43, 48, 119, 145
Colnago............................. 59
Columbia 35, 48-49, 62
Columbus 73, 100, 134-137
Compagnie Parisienne................. 16
Concorezzo......................... 109
Continental..................... 51, 63
Coppi, Fausto 29
Corsa Strada.............. 107, 128, 135
Count Mède de Sivrac................. 14
Crane GS............................ 64
Crank......15, 16, 23, 25, 58, 100, 124, 126
Critérium du Dauphiné Libéré......... 102
Croce d'Aune 26, 117
Crown, Judith........ 5, 39, 42, 43, 48, 119, 145, 146
Csepel Works 122
CycleEurope....................... 125

Cycle Goods Company................ 53
Cyclex............................ 135, 136
Cyclo............................24, 28, 34
Cyclo-cross 138

D

d'Alessandro 101
Davenport, Dwayne 74, 79
Delrin 30-32, 116
Derailleur............23-25, 27-28, 30-34, 45, 48, 60, 62, 65, 67, 74, 76, 80-81, 107, 110, 114, 116-118, 125, 129
   Campagnolo.........27-28, 107, 117-118
   Cyclo........................24, 28, 34
   Gipiemme.........................118
   Huret............... 25, 27-28, 32-33, 48, 65, 76, 129
   Le Cheminaux 23-24
   Ofmega................. 116, 118, 125
   Shimano 60, 62, 65, 116
   Simplex......... 24, 27-28, 30-32, 34, 74, 116, 125
   Suntour 65, 67, 80-81, 110, 114, 116
Deras, Martin 80
Dirt Research 129
Dollar, U.S........................ 113, 138
Dolomites 26
Drais, Baron Karl von 15
Draisine........................... 15
DT spokes........................ 101
Dunelt 54
Dunlop, John 21, 90
Dunning-Kruger Effect............. 122
Dura-Ace 65, 115, 127, 137

E

Earl's Court bicycle show..........54-55
EBM................................ 78
Economic Planning Agency......... 62
Eicma 101
Ejac cables....................... 76
Elan.............................. 90
EL-OS............................ 134
Elrae............................. 54
Elsco Corporation 71-72
Elswick-Hopper................... 54

Why Your Bike Is Made in Asia

Emerson, Jim 86
Engel, Les 54
ESP 123
Euclid 118
Euro 9, 57, 92, 99, 106, 138
Eurobike 101
Europe 9, 14, 24-25, 28-29, 38, 40, 63, 65, 80, 83, 89-90, 101, 138, 140, 142
European Common Market 26
Everest chains and freewheels 97-98
Excelsior 39, 120
Export 61 30

F

Fac Michelin 144
Faggin 99, 100-101, 108-109, 118, 129-130
Faggin, Leandro 99
Faggin, Marcello 99
Falcon 54-56, 141
Federal anti-trust laws 43
Federal Trade Commission 43
Ferry, Jeff 142
Fiamme 48
Fiat 28
Fichtel & Sachs 127-128
Fignon, Laurent 103
Fiorelli 76
Firestone 44-46
Fisher, Gary 110-111
Flandria-Shimano-Carpenter squad 65
Follis 92
Ford 32, 37
Frames 16, 18-19, 22, 31, 41, 56, 58, 76-79, 81-83, 85-88, 91-93, 95-101, 105-109, 116, 119, 120, 124-128, 134-140, 143
    Centurion 80-81
    Cinelli 105
    Faggin 99-101, 109
    Gios 91-92
    Gitane 77-78, 82
    Kestrel 124
    Klein 93
    Maserati 76
    Masi 92, 134
    MKM 92
    Mondonico 109, 134-135

Peugeot 80-81, 116, 125
Pogliaghi 96
Raleigh 78-79
RedLine 85-88
Rossignoli 97-98
Schwinn 119-120
Starley 18-19
Torelli 105, 107, 128, 134-137
Vulcan 92-93
Zunow 128
France 11, 13-14, 17, 22-28, 50, 74, 82, 102, 103, 105, 113, 116, 118, 126, 141, 145, 146
Freewheel 28, 61-67, 76, 82, 90, 97-98, 114-115, 117, 128
    Campagnolo 117
    Cyclo 28
    Everest 97-98
    Regina 90
    Shimano 61-64, 67, 115
    Suntour 65-67
French, Tom 82, 124
Fritz, Al 47-48, 63-64, 120
Fuji 68
Fuller brushes 70
Futura Leggero 136

G

Galli 97-98
Ganna, Luigi 29
Garner, George 43
Gazelle 34, 67
Gérardin, Louis 11
Germany 15, 36, 39, 101, 113, 142
Ghiggini, Francesco 27
Giant 89, 108, 119-122, 141
Giant Manufacturing Co 89
Giffard, Pierre 21
Gios Torino 91-92, 97
Gipiemme 118, 128
Girardengo 54
Giro d'Italia 29, 65, 103, 115, 118
Gitane 8, 73-79, 82
Gloria 29
GM 32
Godefroot, Walter 65
Gormand, Cécile 103
Gormand, Henri 102-103

149

Grand Prix 11, 66-67
Gran Sasso 135-137
Gran Sport 26
Gran Turismo 64, 70
Great Britain 34, 113
Greenville 120-121, 132
Grip Shift, SRAM 122-124
Guerciotti 96, 109-110, 138, 140, 146
Guerciotti, Paolo 96, 109, 140, 146
Gypsy 74

H

Halberstam, David 62
Hampsten, Andy 115
Hanson, Charles 126
Harry Wilson Sales Agency 54
Helen's Cycles 42, 79
Henry, Raymond 24
Herbold, Greg 124
Herlihy, David 17, 145
Hinault, Bernard 126, 145
Hirth joint 141
Hitachi 65
Hogg, Bevil 124
Hontani 128-129
Hubs 26-27, 31, 34, 49, 63, 65, 79, 82, 90, 102, 127, 142, 143
Huffman, George P. 44
Huffman, Horace 44-46
Huffman Manufacturing Company 44
Huffy 44-46, 131
Huffy Scout 46
Hugo 27
Humber 21
Huret 25, 27-28, 31-33, 48, 65, 67, 69, 76, 125, 128-129
Huret, André 25

I

Icarus 118
ICS 92
Ifma 101
Indonesia 142
International Cycle Sport 92
Italian 8-9, 26-27, 31, 76, 78, 81-82, 90, 93, 95-102, 104, 106, 110, 116, 118, 128-129, 133, 135-137, 140, 143

Italian Trade Commission 99
Italvega 96
Italy 8, 14, 16, 23, 25-26, 29, 31, 37, 54, 62, 65, 89, 91, 95, 97-98, 103, 117-118, 135-137, 140, 141, 142, 143
Iwai Seisakusho 65

J

Jackson, Bob 92
Japan 7, 9, 49-50, 57-62, 64, 67, 80, 87-88, 91, 108, 113, 132
Japan Bicycle Promotion Institute 57-58
Joannou, George 54
Johnson, Iver 36
John T. Bill 45
Juarez, Tinker 124
Juy, Lucien 24-25, 32

K

Kageyama 128
Kasten, Linn 85-88, 108
Kawamura 59, 60-61, 87-88, 108, 116
Kestrel 124
KHS 88-89, 108
King Liu 89, 108
Kitching, Ron 92
Klein, Gary 93
Kleyer, Henrick 39

L

Lacomb, Jean-Pierre 104
Lallement, PIerre 16-18, 35
Laufmaschine 15
Lawee, Ben 96
Le Chemineau 23
LeCroix, Mr. 70-71
Legnano 29, 80
Legnano Roma Olimpiade 80
Le Mans 80, 81
LeMay, Curtis 61
LeMond, Greg 103, 145-146
Le Petit Journal 21
Linder-Euro Imports 92
Longo, Jeannie 103
Longsjo, Art 96
Long Yih 141
Look 125-127

Why Your Bike Is Made in Asia

Look Nevada 126
Lo, Tony 121-122
Louvre Accord 113
Lupold, Jim 71

M

Maeda 65
Maertens, Freddy 65
Mafac 13, 14, 31, 74
Magne, Antonin 25
Magni, Fiorenzo 29
Maillard 63, 76, 128
Mannesmann 129, 130
Marra, Claudio 136, 143
Marui 87
Maruka Machinery 59
Marzorati, Marzio 107
Maserati 8, 71, 72, 74, 75, 76
Masi 59, 81, 91, 100, 129, 133, 134, 146
    Tre Volumetrica 134
Masi, Alberto 133
Masi, Faliero 81, 100, 133, 146
Mason, Wes 92
Maule, Cleto 96
Mavic 25, 90, 102, 103, 104, 105, 130
May, Ken 72, 104
McCauley 54
McConnell, Campbell 32
Mektronic 104
Merckx, Eddy 81, 82
Merida 89
Metcalf, Arthur 92
Meteor 55
Meyer, Eugene 16, 17, 18
Michaux, Ernest 16
Miche 144
Michelin 21, 23, 90, 107
Milan 16, 25, 80, 96, 100, 101, 106,
    108, 109
Ministry of International Trade and
    Industry 61
Mirage 135
Mississippi 120, 121, 122, 131, 132
MITI 61
Miyata 65
MKM 92
Modolo 107, 128

Mondonico 109, 110, 118, 129, 134,
    135, 136, 138, 139, 146
Mondonico, Antonio 109, 134, 136, 138,
    146
Mondonico, Mauro 136, 138, 146
Mongoose 144
Montbéliard 23
Monty of Italy 91
Moore's Law 118
Morelon, Daniel 11
Moser, Aldo 96
Motobecane 7, 50
Mountain bike 47, 87, 101, 110, 111,
    113, 118, 120, 123, 124, 127, 129, 130
Murphy Company 79, 80
Murray 46, 48, 58, 120, 121
Murray Ohio Manufacturing Co. 46
Mussolini 135
Mustang, Ford 32
Myers, Jim 78

N

Nemo 136
Nervar 31
Netherlands 142
Neugent, John 89, 129, 130, 137, 146
Nishiki 7, 8, 60, 67, 76, 78, 79, 82
Nissan 65
Nitro Express 134, 135
Nivacrom 134-136
Nivea 29
Nivex 27
Nixon, Richard 50
Normandy hubs 31, 79
Nye, Peter Joffre 5, 21

O

OEM 49, 115, 123, 125, 130, 141
Ofmega 107, 116, 118, 125
Okita, Saburo 62
Olivier brothers 16
Ollivier, Jean-Paul 26
Olmo 76
Olympic Games 15, 58
Open 4 CD 103
Organization of Arab Petroleum
    Exporting Countries 50

Oria.. 135
Osaka... 59, 65, 128
Overman, Albert...................... 17, 19, 20, 24
Ozaki, Nobuo.. 66

P

Packham, Ron.. 11
Padua... 95, 96, 100
Panasonic.. 51, 65
Panel, Joanny.. 23
Paris... 21, 29
Paris–Nice... 103
Paris–Roubaix........................... 29, 65, 105
PBC Distributors....................................... 98
Pedalers West Bike Shop........................ 86
Pedals............... 15-16, 23, 76, 78, 125-127, 140, 143
    Look.. 126-127
    Shimano.. 127
    Torelli................................... 127, 140
Pennsylvania Rubber............................... 54
Penny-farthing... 18
Pep Boys.. 69
Peugeot.............. 7, 9, 11-13, 22-23, 25-26, 30-31, 34, 50, 58, 61, 67, 76, 78-82, 106, 116-117, 125
    PFC10Z.. 125
    PX10.. 81-82
    PX10S... 81
    PY10FC.. 116
    UO8..................... 12-13, 30-31, 61, 67
Playrite Bicycle Supply Company......53-56
Plaza Accord... 113
Plunger... 28
Pogliaghi, Sante.................................. 90, 96
Poland... 142
Pollentier, Michel..................................... 65
Pope, Albert....................... 17, 35-38, 49
Portugal... 142
Positron... 114
Pranke, Chuck... 11
Predator... 108, 119
ProCycle.. 125

Q

QUARQ... 124
Quick-release.. 26

R

RadioBike.. 45
Raleigh............. 7, 12, 30, 34, 49, 50, 54-57, 59, 67, 78-79, 82
Rebour, Daniel.................................. 33, 34
RedLine................................ 86-88, 107-108
RedLine Engineering............................... 87
Reg... 105
Regina... 90, 97
Repack... 110
Reynolds............. 18, 21-22, 34, 79, 81, 138
Rigida..................................... 31, 76, 90, 102
Rims.......... 13-14, 17-19, 25, 31, 37, 39, 44, 48, 90, 102, 104, 107, 140, 143
    Ambrosio................................. 102, 107
    Fiamme... 48
    Mavic...................... 25, 90, 102, 107
    Rigida.. 31
    Torelli..................................... 104, 140
Ritchey, Tom.. 110
Roadmaster.. 46
Rockefeller, John D................................. 36
RockShox... 123
Romana... 78
Roma Olimpliade..................................... 80
Ross, Albert.. 46
Ross Bicycles...................................... 46, 47
Rossignol Group..................................... 124
Rossignoli... 96, 97
Ross, Sherwood....................................... 46
Rover... 18
Royal Scot.. 55
Royce Union............................. 57, 59, 86
Rubenson, Paul.. 37
Ruta del Sol race...................................... 65

S

SAB.. 106, 128
Sachs............................. 123, 125, 127-130
Sachs, Ernst... 127
Sachs-Huret................................... 125, 128
Safety bicycle... 18
Salomon.. 104
Sapo pumps... 140
SARA.. 116
Saunier, Louis Baudry de....................... 14

Why Your Bike Is Made in Asia

Schwinn 5, 7, 9, 12, 33, 35-36, 38-44, 46-48, 51, 53-54, 57, 59, 61, 63-64, 73-74, 79, 82-83, 85, 86, 91, 101-102, 108, 110, 111, 118-122, 124, 132-133, 145
Schwinn, Ed 44, 119-122, 132-133
Schwinn, Frank V 40, 44, 48, 73, 119, 120
Schwinn, Frank W. 39, 41-42, 44
Schwinn, Ignaz 35-36, 38-39, 41, 119
Scout 46
Scrambler 119
Sears 36, 39, 41, 46, 48, 132
Sedis 128
Seidler, Rudy 67, 72
Sekai 68
Selle Royal 105
Sequoia 110
Service Cycle 89, 129
Shimano 49, 57-58, 60-67, 79, 87, 101, 105, 114-117, 123-124, 127-130, 132, 137, 141
Shimano, Keizo 62
Shimano, Shozaburo 61
Shimano, Shozo 62
Shimano, Yoshizo (Yoshi) 63
Shimonoseki 64
Shingles 139
Simplex 24-25, 27-28, 30-34, 48, 60, 67, 74, 116, 118, 125
Simpson, Tom 81
Single-tube tire 36-38, 40-41
Sinyard, Michael 89-90, 105, 110
SIS 114-117, 129
S.J. Clarks Cables 105
SL 100, 134-136
Slant parallelogram derailleurs 66, 114-115, 117-118
SLX 134-135
Smart Cycles 138
Solida 31, 125
Southern California Bicycle Association 54
Spada 135, 137
Spain 26, 65, 142
Spalding 20
Spalding, A. G. 36
SPD 127
Specialized 89-90, 110, 122
Specialized Touring Tire 90-91
Spirex 27

SRAM 122-124, 130, 132, 141
Standard Station 69-71
Stanek, Alex 138
Starley 18-19, 23
Stella 28
St. Etienne 25, 31
Steyr-Puch 48
Stiletto 137
Sting-Ray 47-48, 73, 85, 119, 120
Stronglight 25, 81, 125
Stumpjumper 110
Sturmey-Archer 34, 49, 62
Sugino 60
Sukosha Bicycle Company 88
SunRace 141
SunTour 65-67, 80-81, 110, 114-116, 129, 141
Super Balloon Tire Bicycle 40
Super Strada 136
Suzue 79
Svelto 65
Syncro 117

T

T.A. 111
TA cotterless cranks 110
Taiwan 47, 88-89, 106, 108, 116, 119-121, 123, 127, 132, 137-138, 140-144
Taiwanese 88, 108, 111, 116, 143
Takai 57-59
Takai, Kazuo 57
Takara 68
Takei 63
Ten Speed Drive 109
Terront, Charles 21-22
The Penguin 45
The Rail 45
Thévenet, Bernard 82
Thompson, Robert W. 21
Throckmorton, Helen 42
Thron 134-135
Thun 129
TIG 85, 87-88, 93, 108
Tiger Group 124
Tillinghast, Pardon 37
Time Sport 124, 126

153

Tipo Roma 80
Titanio 137
Toccata 138
Tokyo 58, 59, 61
Torelli 96, 98, 102, 104-108,
  114, 127-130, 134-141
  Alu-Wing 135
  Brianza 135-137
  EL-OS 134
  Futura Leggero 136
  Gran Sasso 135-137
  Nemo747 136
  Nitro Express 135
  Spada 135
  Super Strada 136
  Thron 134-135
  Titanio 137
  Toccata 138
Torpado 95, 96
Toshiba 65
Tour de France 14, 23, 25, 27, 82, 103,
  105, 118, 126, 145, 146
Trek 82-83, 92-93, 122, 124
Trentin, Pierre 11
Triumph 34
TSDI 109
TSX 134
Turbo 90-91

U

UAW 108, 119-120
Ultegra 137
Ultra-Torque 141
Unicrown fork 87
Union spokes 76
Uniroyal 37
United Auto Workers 46, 108, 119
United Bicycle Sales 12, 30, 67, 73, 76
United Cycle Supply 105
United States 19, 22, 34, 37-38, 48, 50,
  108, 113, 131, 133, 138, 142
Univega 96
Universal 14
U.S. Government's Consumer Protection
  Safety Commission 45
U.S. Rubber 37, 38, 40
U.S. Supreme Court 43

V

Varsity 33, 48, 51, 61, 63, 119
Veloce 135
Velocipede 16
Velodrome 11
Veneto 31, 100, 109
Ventura 69, 70-72, 76
Vespa 28
Vicini 106, 128
Victor 19-20
Vietnam 142
Vittoria 26, 101, 105, 140
Vitus 116, 127
Vulcan 92

W

Walmart 131
Webco 85
Weiner, Mitchell 67, 80
Weinmann 14, 59, 76
West Coast Cycle 54-55, 57, 59-60,
  67, 76
Western Auto 45-46, 49, 59, 62-63
Western States Imports 68, 80, 88, 113,
  122
West Germany 113
Wheels 14-15, 17-18, 21, 25, 31, 45, 48,
  51, 53, 76, 82, 85, 93, 104, 107, 114, 128,
  140, 143
  Ambrosio 107
  Mavic 104
  Torelli 140
Whizzer 54
Whizzer Motor Company 54
Windsor/Windsor Professional 73
Wolber 90, 102
Workman, Daniel 141
World-brand bikes 51
World Championships 28, 103
Wright, Tony 106

X

XTR 130

Why Your Bike Is Made in Asia

Y

Yen 113, 116
Yoko 65
Yokota 129
Yom Kippur War 50

Z

ZAP 104
Zell-Chilmark 133
Zell, Sam 133
Zeus 31, 128
Zipp 124
Zona 135
Zunow 128-129

www.ingramcontent.com/pod-product-compliance
Lightning Source LLC
Chambersburg PA
CBHW021004090426
42738CB00007B/640